serene cuisine

serene cuisine

TRADITIONAL YOGIC RECIPES FOR THE MIND & BODY

Nicky Moona

Sterling Publishing Co., Inc.
New York

Library of Congress Cataloging-in-Publication Data

Moona, Nicky.
 Serene cuisine : traditional yogic recipes for the mind & body / Nicky Moona.
    p. cm.
 Includes index.
 ISBN 1-4027-1342-8
 1. Vegetarian cookery. 2. Cookery, Yoga. I. Title.

TX837.M6665 2004
641.5'636--dc22

                              2004016219

2 4 6 8 10 9 7 5 3 1

Published by Sterling Publishing Co., Inc.
387 Park Avenue South, New York, NY 10016
© 2004 by Nicky Moona
Distributed in Canada by Sterling Publishing
c/o Canadian Manda Group, 165 Dufferin Street
Toronto, Ontario, Canada M6K 3H6
Distributed in Great Britain by Chrysalis Books Group PLC
The Chrysalis Building, Bramley Road, London W10 6SP, England
Distributed in Australia by Capricorn Link (Australia) Pty. Ltd.
P.O. Box 704, Windsor, NSW 2756, Australia

Photography: Theresa Raffetto Photography
Design: Gretchen Scoble Design

Sterling ISBN 1-4027-1342-8

This book is inspired by and dedicated
to my mother, Sandhya, who has taught
me some of life's most essential lessons
and the ability to be healthy and happy,
both physically and spiritually.
Mum, thank you for your selfless
and everlasting love and support.

Acknowledgments

I would like to express my gratitude to the following people:

Special thanks to my family—my mother and my father,
Mahendra, for all their love and encouragement; and my brother, Vivek,
whose passion for food inspired my culinary creations.

Heartfelt thanks to my friends—Supriva Gaitonde, Wasan Al Saleh,
Lorian Lombardi, Ingrid Almonte, Suli Bhanji, Suku Polavaram, and Sharon Lewis,
who have all appreciated my cooking over the years and supported me in
the process of getting this book published.

And personal thanks to my terrific editor Danielle Truscott,
inimitable food stylist William Smith,
and photographer extraordinaire Theresa Raffetto.

Contents

Introduction

Yoga is not only a program of exercise that benefits the body as well as the spirit but also a way of life that is full of joy, serenity, and good health.

Although yoga exercise is very popular among those pursuing a healthy lifestyle, the yogic diet is not, even though it is equally important. One reason for this discrepancy is that people think the food is dull and boring. But nothing could be farther from the truth!

This book provides a simple guide to preparing delicious food that is wholesome and nutritious and that also conforms to yoga discipline. Each recipe features a corresponding yoga posture, or asana, and the recipes all address three main principles of yoga:

❖ *Physical Body*—A well-balanced meal and regular exercise result in a healthy body.
❖ *Mind*—What you eat becomes your mind. As is the food, so is your mind.
❖ *Spirit*—Purity of the inner nature depends on the purity of food.

The yogic diet's potential for physical and mental transformation and its accessibility make it an ideal program for a healthy existence. It can help you to

❖ *monitor body weight*
❖ *boost energy*
❖ *improve concentration and memory*
❖ *revitalize the body*

❖ *strengthen the immune system*
❖ *aid digestion, absorption, and elimination*
❖ *improve sleep*
❖ *help release and manage stress*

This diet is for people who want to be healthy and happy. And who in the world would want anything different?

Yoga and Yogic Food

YOGA

Yoga is an ancient system of discipline that helps people to develop mind and body and to reach a higher level of spirituality. It has been a tradition in India for more than three thousand years and is independent of any religious or secular institution. It does not lay down rules; it is simply a way of life. Yoga is union: the union of the mind and the body, of the conscious and the subconscious. There are many paths to achieve it. Some of the most common techniques include Karma Yoga (the yoga of service), Raja Yoga (the yoga of mind), Jnana Yoga (the yoga of wisdom and knowledge), Bhakti Yoga (the yoga of devotion), Kundalini Yoga (the yoga of energy), and Hatha Yoga (the yoga of posture and breath). All yoga techniques require healthy eating habits and recommend the consumption of yogic food.

YOGIC FOOD

For centuries, yoga has focused on the development of an eating philosophy based on a wholesome diet. Its principles of good eating are based on effective techniques that help to maintain a strong and healthy body, a stress-free mind, and a positive spirituality. The traditional holistic yogic diet is completely vegetarian. It is based on the idea that foods must be consumed in their most natural forms in order to realize their true benefits. The yogic belief is that several health disorders can be traced to faulty nutrition and poor diet. Removing or reducing the consumption of animal products can help reduce the chances of developing diseases, including serious illnesses such as heart-related problems and certain forms of cancer. A vegetarian yogic diet ensures the proper functioning of the whole digestive system: absorption, assimilation, and elimination. The diet also contains high amounts of fiber and antioxidants. The benefits of a well-balanced vegetarian diet should not be underestimated.

"YOU ARE WHAT YOU EAT"

What does that statement mean to you? To most people, it simply says that the vitamins, carbohydrates, and proteins in food build cells, blood, and bones in the body. In yoga, however, "You are what you eat" has a far more subtle and powerful meaning. Food is known to directly influence consciousness and feelings. It can induce bliss or anger, contentment or restlessness, thoughts of the sacred or thoughts of the profane. The quality of the food you eat literally creates your state of mind, emotions, and consciousness. The teachings of yoga advocate a vegetarian diet with special emphasis on foods that bring peace to body, mind, and spirit.

The highest form of duty to oneself is the partaking of foods that are directly beneficial to health. What you eat and the state of mind you eat in have direct impact on your health. The state of your health is dependent not only on what you choose to eat but also on what you choose not to eat. Being aware of the types of foods you consume—in terms of both benefits and ill effects—is very important.

A traditional yogic diet consists of fruits, vegetables, whole grains, and legumes. Fresh fruit and vegetable juices possess curative properties and are used to treat many common ailments naturally. Dairy products such as milk and yogurt are also recommended. According to yogic tradition, milk is one of the purest foods.

FUNDAMENTAL FOOD DISTINCTIONS: SATTVIC, RAJASIC, AND TAMASIC FOODS

SATTVIC FOOD—EAT MOST

Sattvic means "pure essence." A Sattvic diet includes the consumption of pure foods that lead to the essence of true health. This is the purest form of the yogic diet and most suitable for serious yoga followers. It not only nourishes the body but calms and purifies the mind to maintain a peaceful state, enabling the body to function at its maximum potential while attaining spiritual growth. This type of food is all natural and easily digestible. It generates vitality, vigor, energy, and mental alertness; increases strength; eliminates fatigue; and enhances spirituality, peace, and tranquillity.

The human body has fundamental requirements: fats, proteins, carbohydrates, vitamins and minerals, fiber, and water. The Sattvic diet satisfies these requirements by including the majority of fresh fruits and vegetables, whole grains and unrefined foods, legumes, nuts and seeds, milk and milk products, and natural sweeteners.

Vegetables and fruits are rich in vital nutrients that are best absorbed when they are fresh and ripe for the season. To ensure micronutrient-dense foods (foods rich in vitamins and minerals), the larger part of the Sattvic diet should consist of a variety of fresh vegetables, herbs, and fruits, especially in a color range of red, purple, green, orange, and yellow.

Whole grains and foods made from unrefined grains are an intrinsic part of the Sattvic diet and provide the dietary fiber and carbohydrates needed by the body to provide fuel for movement. The best high-carbohydrate foods include whole-grain wheat, barley, corn, millet, oat, and unpolished rice.

Legumes, nuts, seeds, and milk products—proteins—are the primal life substance the cells need to build and repair our bodies. The Sattvic diet depends heavily on them. Protein-rich foods include legumes such as moong lentils, cereals, all beans, split peas, and bean sprouts. The best combinations of fats and protein come from nuts such as almonds, pistachios, peanuts, and cashews. Milk and milk products should be organic and nonfat or low-fat; they are best consumed in moderation.

Natural sweeteners such as honey and unrefined raw sugars are Sattvic and good for the health.

Spices are used only in small quantities for Sattvic consumption and are recommended for their therapeutic value and flavor. The generous use of spices is a characteristic of the Rajasic and Tamasic diets.

Sattvic foods are highly recommended for the relief of stress and the realization of a peaceful state of mind. Following a strict Sattvic diet is believed to be the highest attainment in the yogic food philosophy and is followed by dedicated yogis.

RAJASIC FOOD—EAT MODERATELY

Rajasic food signifies a "can-do" attitude, but it creates imbalance, overstimulates the body, and causes restlessness. It is believed to generate anxiety, anger, violence, greed, sorrow, pain, lust, egotism, and stress. However, it also generates excitement, fantasies, sensuality, sexuality, and the energy we need to accomplish, create, and achieve. We require a certain amount of Rajasic energy to survive; it enables us to keep pace with the changing world around us.

For understandable reasons, Rajasic foods are recommended for only moderate or occasional consumption. These include all spicy, hot, bitter, sour, gaseous, and pungent foods, which are not as easily digestible as Sattvic foods. Examples include salted, chemically processed foods; bitter, sour, and gaseous foods such as toor lentils, white urad lentils, black and green gram, chickpeas, and soybeans; hot spices such as chilies and black pepper; and stimulants such as onion and garlic, tea, coffee, tobacco, soda, chocolate, and refined sugars.

Rajasic foods are recommended for people who require high levels of energy or for people with high levels of physical activity. These foods are especially appropriate for the winter season.

TAMASIC FOOD—EAT LEAST

Tamasic foods benefit neither the mind nor the body. Under their influence, the body's resistance to disease is destroyed, and the mind is filled with pessimism and the negative emotions of greed, anger, and impure thoughts. This type of food is very difficult to digest and generates the least amount of energy, often leading to dullness and lethargy. Tamasic foods enhance laziness, compulsion, suffering, depression, and dullness of the mind. Tamasic foods are impure, stale, fermented, highly processed, and addictive. They include meat, fish, eggs, intoxicants, alcohol, and stale food (food kept for more than twenty-four hours). Processed, canned, and frozen foods are Tamasic, as are foods containing preservatives, chemical additives, and artificial flavors and colors, and reheated and deep-fried foods. These foods consume large amounts of energy while being digested and are believed to create antagonistic feelings. The body feels heavy and the mind unfocused and uninspired. Tamasic foods are anathema to the basic goal of yoga: the union of mind and body.

It is best to avoid Tamasic foods if you are interested in vitality and spiritual growth.

SOME IMPORTANT RECOMMENDATIONS

EATING SCHEDULE

According to yoga, it is best to eat four times a day at four-hour intervals. Ideally, the first meal of the day would be consumed at sunrise and the last meal at sunset, thus bringing you into perfect harmony with nature. This shifting schedule, however, can be difficult to integrate with an active lifestyle. A good routine is to have breakfast at 8 a.m., lunch at noon, a snack at 4 p.m., and the last meal by 8 p.m.

In general, try to eat and drink within two hours of waking up. In addition to these four main meals a day, you can snack—but strictly on fruits and juices, preferably lime juice. Snacks should be light and easily digestible.

THE IMPORTANCE OF BREAKFAST

You've heard it before, and it's true in the yogic diet too: Breakfast is the most important meal of the day. Since you haven't eaten for almost twelve hours, the body feels fatigued until it is properly nourished. Without breakfast, you can fall prey to lack of concentration and low energy.

THE IMPORTANCE OF DRINKING WATER

Yoga recommends the consumption of eight glasses of water a day. Drink a half glass of warm water first thing in the morning, one glass thirty minutes before each meal, and another glass an hour after each meal. (Do not drink water with a meal.) This routine essentially fulfills the daily requirements.

HOW MUCH TO EAT

It is not just the quality of food consumed that is important but also the quantity. According to yoga, after a meal the stomach should be half filled with food (including liquids), a quarter filled with water (to be taken thirty minutes before and one hour after meals), and a quarter empty (for the proper movement and digestion of food and for the formation of gases).

A good way to know if your stomach is full is to listen to your hunger pangs. If you really feel hungry four hours after a meal, you have consumed the right quantity of food.

FAT AND OIL CONSUMPTION

The body needs fat, and it is available in both visible and invisible forms. The visible form of fat is found in foods such as oil, butter, and margarine. The invisible form is found in items such as nuts and milk products. The body requires small quantities of fat because it helps in the absorption of fat-soluble vitamins such as vitamins A, D, E, and K. The yogic diet allows the consumption of two teaspoons of oil per day.

STATE OF MIND WHILE EATING

In yoga, perfection is attained through control over the mind. Central to this state is the belief that one should focus on a single activity at a time, giving it total attention, whether that activity is eating, studying, cooking, or brushing the teeth. The concept of "silence"—in which you learn to live in the present moment and concentrate on what you are doing—is very important. While eating, your mind should be totally focused on the act of eating. You should not talk, and no thoughts should be entertained while you eat. (This is very difficult to achieve! Alternatively, you might try to consciously generate a happy and positive environment during mealtimes: positive thoughts, conversation, and emotions.) According to yogic principles, you maximize the assimilation and absorption of food when you eat with concentration and in peace.

COOKING WITH LOVE

When you cook for your family and friends, it is important to be in a positive frame of mind. The ancient Indian texts have pointed out that the vibration of the cook's feelings affects the quality of the food. When cooking, focus on the preparation and make the meal a settled, conscious event rather than something you're throwing together under pressure. Give yourself time to enjoy the simple act of smelling the spices, feeling the textures, playing with the colors. If your kids, friends, spouse, or partner like to help, get them involved. However it works for you, make food preparation a happy time. Your positive thoughts and feelings will transform the meal into a true feast.

Spices

USING SPICES FOR THERAPEUTIC BENEFIT
Spices are an intrinsic part of Indian cooking, and most are known to possess therapeutic and healing properties. Yoga suggests that they be used never in excess but in small quantities to derive the most benefit from their health-enhancing effects. What's more, the exotic colors and heady aromas of spices can elevate a dish from the ordinary to a sublime feast for the senses. This cookbook will start you out with suggestions for using spices that are especially balancing for the mind and body, as well as with tips on how to use them.

ASAFETIDA POWDER/HING (SATTVIC)
Asafetida is a dried resinlike substance obtained from the rhizomes of several species of ferule, or giant fennel. Its name is derived from the Persian *aza* (resin), and the Latin *fetida* (stinking), so the name describes its most obvious attributes. Ferula are odorous plants that grow to heights of between six and twelve feet. They have soft-centered stems and finely toothed leaves and produce clusters of yellow flowers. When the stems and roots are cut, a milky liquid exudes, which then dries to form asafetida. It is used in ground powder form. In western and southern India, asafetida flavors pulses and vegetable dishes, pickles and sauces. It should always be used sparingly. The pungent, bitter smell and taste disappear when cooked, leaving behind an onionlike flavor.

THERAPEUTIC VALUE: *Asafetida has antispasmodic properties and aids in digestion.*

TURMERIC POWDER/HALDI (SATTVIC)
A member of the ginger family, turmeric is cultivated widely in India, China, Taiwan, Indonesia, Vietnam, and the Philippines and is used throughout southern Asia. It is the underground rhizome of a robust perennial plant that grows to a height of about three feet. Although available fresh, the rhizome is most often sold dried and ground to a powder. It adds a warm, mild aroma and distinctive yellow color to foods. Turmeric can stain fabrics and other materials, so handle it carefully.

THERAPEUTIC VALUE: *Turmeric is a heating spice for the body. This all-around wonder spice possesses anti-inflammatory properties and is a powerful antioxidant. Even a teaspoon of it has medicinal value. Using it as a seasoning agent in food makes good sense.*

RED CHILIES/MIRCHI (RAJASIC)

Chilies are members of the capsicum family (as are sweet peppers), and they come in all shapes, sizes, and colors. There are over two hundred different types of chilies grown in all parts of the tropics. Indigenous to Central and South America and the West Indies, they are now cultivated in India, Mexico, China, Japan, Indonesia, and Thailand. Chilies have little aroma but vary in taste from mild to fiery hot. Hot red chilies, such as cayenne peppers, are used in cuisines around the world to spice up many savory dishes. They enhance the bland flavor of staple foods such as rice in India and Southeast Asia, beans and corn in Mexico, and cassava in South America. After being harvested, red chilies are dried in the sun and may be left whole, crushed into flakes, or ground into powder. Do not touch the eyes or any cuts when handling red chilies.

THERAPEUTIC VALUE: *Dried chilies contain beta-carotene and vitamin C. Red chili peppers in any form should be used in minute quantities for their Sattvic benefits and not consumed in excess.*

CORIANDER/DHANIYA (SATTVIC)

Originally from North Africa but now cultivated in southern Europe as well as the Middle and Far East, India, and the Americas, coriander is popular in cuisines worldwide. It grows from one to three feet tall and bears small clusters of tiny white or pink flowers. All parts of the plant are used for different cuisines in different ways. The root is used fresh in Thai curries and other Southeast Asian dishes. The fresh leaves (also known as cilantro or Chinese parsley) are used in Southeast Asia, the Middle East, Spain, Portugal, and Mexico. In northern Europe, the seeds are used for flavoring gin or as an ingredient in pickling spices. On the Indian subcontinent, both the seeds and the leaves are essential ingredients in curries.

THERAPEUTIC VALUE: *Coriander is known to be a powerful aid to digestion and helps to prevent infection in wounds and to combat allergies.*

CUMIN/JEERA (SATTVIC)

Originally from the Nile Valley, cumin has been grown in India, Egypt, Saudi Arabia, and Mediterranean countries. It needs a warm climate and thrives best in sandy, calcium-rich soil. The plant grows to a height of about one foot, and fruits appear after two months. The spice comes from the seeds, which are used both whole and in powder form. Cumin powder, a rich brown color, is made from cumin seeds that have been dry-roasted and then ground. The smell of cumin is quite pronounced— strong and heavy, with acrid or warm depths. It tastes slightly bitter, sharp, and warm, and its pungent flavor persists for some time. Both sautéing and roasting make the aroma and flavor of cumin come alive.

THERAPEUTIC VALUE: *Cumin is a cooling spice. It is supposed to aid digestion and help flush toxins out of the body.*

FENNEL SEEDS/SAUF (SATTVIC)

Fennel is native to southern Europe but is now cultivated for export in Germany, Italy, France, Russia, the Middle East, and India. A perennial that grows up to four feet tall, it has an erect, bright green stem. The yellow flowers grow in dense, compact clusters. The fruits, which are about one-half inch long, are oval and ridged. The seed heads are harvested just before the fruit ripens. Fennel seeds are sweetish in taste and work as fabulous flavor enhancers. They also have healing properties.

THERAPEUTIC VALUE: *Fennel seeds are a cooling spice and are believed to help cure stomach maladies. They are extremely good for digestion. In India, eating a few fennel seeds after a meal is a common practice.*

MUSTARD SEEDS/RAI (SATTVIC)

Black mustard is a native of Eurasia. Cultivated as a field crop in Europe for centuries, it has been used since ancient times. A well-known oil seed, mustard is a small annual plant that thrives in temperate climates and grows up to a height of three feet. The fruit is a pod of about one inch long that contains seeds. Dry mustard seeds are small, round, and dark brown or grayish brown. As whole seeds, they have no smell, but when pounded and moistened with water, they emit a pungent odor. The taste of mustard seeds is bitter.

THERAPEUTIC VALUE: *Mustard not only stimulates the appetite but also has digestive, laxative, antiseptic, and circulative stimulant properties.*

GENERAL TIPS FOR COOKING WITH SPICES

✤ *Spices should be used in small quantities for maximum therapeutic (Sattvic) benefit. They become Rajasic when used in excess.*

✤ *Most spices are potent, so a little goes a long way. You want to enhance the flavor of the food, not overpower the dish.*

✤ *When blending several spices in a dish, experiment to find combinations with other spices and different foods that appeal to you. You'll find your own favorite ways to use them. Be adventurous!*

✤ *Look for organic, nonirradiated spices. These can be found at any Indian grocery store. To locate a grocery store near you, search the Internet—or buy spices online.*

✤ *Store spices in airtight containers, away from heat and light.*

TRADITIONAL YOGIC GRAINS

BASMATI RICE (BASMATI CHAVAL) — THE HOLY GRAIN

In India, from Vedic times to the present, a spiritual aura has surrounded the preparation and consumption of basmati rice. Some consider it sacred, often using it in offerings to gods. The most aromatic of all rice grains, it has an unmistakable fragrance (basmati means "the queen of fragrance"). This Sattvic grain can be prepared in several ways and is often combined with herbs, vegetables, and spices. The grains of basmati rice are long and silky to the touch and are available in both white and brown varieties. White basmati is very easy to digest and is a very highly regarded component of the yogic diet as it is consumed with almost every meal. It is also known in ayurveda for its cleansing and healing properties. Brown rice, although not as easily digestible as white, has a higher fiber content.

Traditional Preparation

Rinse the rice in cold water and drain it several times before placing it in a cooking pot with enough cold water to cover. Allow it to soak for 15 to 30 minutes.

NOTE: If you do not soak the rice first, cook one part rice with two parts water. Be advised, however, that soaked rice can use less water, for example, one cup rice and one and three-quarter cups water. Bring the rice and water to a boil, cover with a tight lid, and reduce the heat to a simmer. Don't lift the lid or stir the rice as it cooks. When rice is cooking it expands to form steam tunnels. If cooking is interrupted, the rice will not cook evenly and the result will be a combination of burned and/or underdone rice. Allow the rice to cook for 15 to 20 minutes. The rice should not be mushy and stuck together. Each grain should come out firm and separate.

Alternative Method

Add one handful of rinsed rice per person to a large pot of boiling water, using more water than can be absorbed (you don't need to use a measuring cup). Boil 10 minutes or until the rice has finished cooking. It is not necessary to cover the pot. Drain the rice in a colander.

NOTE: Do not add cold water to rice that is already cooking as it makes the rice difficult to digest. Do not add salt until the rice has partially or completely cooked. Most rice recipes suggest that you add salt at the beginning, but yoga says that the salt actually affects the temperature of the cooking process and can adversely affect the potential benefits of the rice. Use salt moderately and mix it in after the rice has half-cooked or preferably after it has finished cooking.

WHEAT (GEHU)

Like rice, wheat is an ancient grain that has been a staple in Indian and yogic cuisine for more than five thousand years. Wheat recipes from the Vedas, ancient holy texts, are still used today. Wheat is cooling in energy and is a vital, moist, sweet grain rich in vitamins and minerals. In its natural, unrefined state, wheat features a host of valuable nutrients. Flatbread made from whole-wheat flour, known as roti or chapati, is an integral part of every homemade meal. Yoga encourages the consumption of whole wheat as this provides the dietary fiber and good carbohydrates that all bodies require. Whole wheat comes in many different forms. The most commonly used in Indian yogic food include wheat flour, cracked wheat (Dalia), and semolina (Suji).

Traditional Preparation: Roti/Chapati

Step 1: Prepare the dough: Measure the whole-wheat flour into a large bowl. Make a well in the center and pour in a stream of water (Example: Mix 2½ cups whole-wheat flour and 1 cup room-temperature water to form a dough that will make bread for six.) Use one hand to mix the flour and water in a rotating motion from the center of the bowl outward, until the dough is moist enough to be gathered into a rough mass. Wet hands and continue working the dough until the mixture leaves the side of the bowl and has become a nonsticky, kneadable dough. When the dough is kneaded, it will be elastic and silky smooth. To test the dough, press it lightly with a fingertip. If it springs back, it is ready to rest. Resting allows the dough to relax and absorb the water. In warm climates the dough should rest for 15 minutes; in cold climates, for 30 minutes. Cover it with a clean damp towel to prevent the dough from drying out.

Step 2: Roll out the dough: Divide the dough into peach-size balls. On a lightly floured surface, flatten one ball of dough with your hand. Using a rolling pin, roll the dough into a thin, round patty, about 6 inches in diameter. Roll from the center, turning the patty several times and using a little roti flour from a separate plate for dusting the dough to prevent it from sticking. Try to make the edges slightly thinner than the center. As you cook each roti, start rolling out the next, rather than shape all of the roti at one time.

Step 3: Cook the roti: Preheat a cast-iron tawa/pan over medium heat. Place the rolled dough on the palm of one hand and flip it over onto the tawa. When the color changes on the top and bubbles appear, turn it over. Using kitchen tongs, remove the roti from the tawa and hold the half-cooked roti directly over a flame. It will puff up immediately. Turn it quickly to flame-bake the other side. Repeat a few times, making sure that the edges are well cooked.

Step 4: Serve hot, either completely dry or topped with a minute amount of ghee (page 28).

BARLEY (JOWAR)

Possibly one of the oldest grains in the world, barley has been cultivated in India since the Vedic period. It can be used either whole or ground to flour in different food preparations. Its attributes are coolness, lightness, and dryness. It acts as a laxative and is known to help relieve constipation. It is a nutritious food for infants as well as adults.

Traditional Preparation: Jowar Roti

Step 1: Prepare the dough: Use the same method as for whole-wheat roti.

Step 2: Roll out the dough: Divide the dough into peach-size balls. On a lightly floured, flat surface, pat one ball of dough with your palm, instead of a rolling pin, into a thick, round patty, about 3 to 4 inches in diameter.
NOTE: This bread is much smaller and thicker than the whole-wheat roti.

Step 3: Cook the roti: Preheat a cast-iron tawa/pan over medium heat. Place the rolled dough on the palm of one hand and flip it over onto the tawa. Cook for 1 minute or until the color changes on the top and bubbles appear. Using tongs, turn it quickly to the other side and cook for another minute. The roti is ready when both sides are lightly brown.

Step 4: Serve hot, either completely dry or topped with a minute amount of ghee.

MILLET (BAJRA)

Millet is the third most commonly used grain after rice and wheat in yogic cuisine. This tiny yellow to reddish round grain is heating in energy and is light and dry in its most natural form. It is gluten-free and can be used whole or ground to flour for food preparations. The versatility of millet is boundless. It is often mixed with other flours to form flatbreads, cooked to make a hot cereal, or mixed with vegetables or rice. It is high in protein, vitamin B, copper, iron, magnesium, calcium, and fiber.

Traditional Preparation: Bajra Roti
Step 1: Prepare the dough: Use the same method as for whole-wheat roti.

Step 2: Roll out the dough: Divide the dough into peach-size balls. On a lightly floured, flat surface, pat one ball of dough with your palm, instead of a rolling pin, into a thick, round patty, about 3 to 4 inches in diameter.
NOTE: This bread is much smaller and thicker than the whole-wheat roti.

Step 3: Cook the roti: Preheat a cast-iron tawa/pan over medium heat. Place the rolled dough on the palm of one hand and flip it over onto the tawa. Cook for 1 minute or until the color changes on the top and bubbles appear. Using tongs, turn it quickly to the other side and cook for another minute. The roti is ready when both sides are lightly brown.

Step 4: Serve hot, either completely dry or topped with a minute amount of ghee.

MAIZE/CORN (MAKKAI)
Native to India, this wonderful grain is used as a vegetable or a flour. Like millet and barley, corn is used by a large portion of the world's population, especially in rural India. Classified as seeds of cereal plants, they are small and hard and have low water content. Corn is a warm grain that is rich in sugar, fiber, and carbohydrates. Low in gluten, it is used for making flatbreads. Given its benefits, yoga recommends eating and cooking corn in any form: corn on the cob, kernels, grains/cereals, and flour/cornmeal.

Traditional Preparation: Makkai Roti
Use the same method as for Millet/Bajra roti.

NOTE: There are several other equally beneficial grains that are nontraditional yogic food (not mentioned in the vedas or the holy books) that can be adapted to the cuisine. Some of these include oats, couscous, rye, triticale (a crossbreed of wheat and rye), quinoa, and amaranth.

MILK AND MILK PRODUCTS

MILK (DOODH)—THE HEALING FOOD FOR HUMANS

Since the Vedic period, milk has been known as the "promoter of life," a "potent nectar" for humans. According to yoga, milk is a complete food in and of itself, and some of the ancient sages, who are said to have lived very long and healthy lives, used to live on a diet of milk, fruits, and vegetables. In its original state it is Sattvic in nature and has been used widely but not wisely. According to yoga guidelines, milk should never be used with foods such as cooked vegetables, salt, fish, or meat, nor should it be used with meals as an accompanying beverage.

Avoid excessive use of milk; consume it in small quantities and use natural or organic, low-fat or nonfat milk for its health benefits. It may be combined with dried or cooked fruits in the form of a milk shake or sweet dessert. It is best consumed cool or warm, by itself. Milk helps to cool the body, calm the mind, and relieve anxiety or stress and restlessness. Milk contains many valuable nutrients, including proteins and amino acids, carbohydrates, fats, essential fatty acids, and calcium.

INDIAN CLARIFIED BUTTER (GHEE)

Ghee is one of the most ancient Sattvic foods. Yoga places ghee, or clarified butter, at the top of the oily foods list, as it has the healing benefits of butter without butter's impurities (lactose, saturated fat, and milk solids). Ghee is good for all body types and synergizes with food nutrients, nourishing the body. Ghee lubricates the connective tissues and promotes flexibility. Traditionally, the preparation has been used to promote memory and intelligence, enhance digestion, and bolster the immune system. Ghee should be used in moderation for its health benefits, as excess use can have a reverse effect.

Traditional Preparation

The traditional process for making ghee involves boiling milk and allowing it to cool, then skimming the cream off the top. This has to be done several times until you have accumulated enough cream. This cream, also called malai, or butter, is then cooked gently over medium heat until it becomes a clear golden liquid. The lactose and other milk solids that coagulate are meticulously removed. This process also evaporates most of the natural water content, making ghee light, pure, and resistant to spoilage. Ghee can stay pure indefinitely without refrigeration. Alternatively, you can find ghee in any Indian grocery store.

YOGURT (DAHI)

Yogurt, dahi, or curd, known as the "protector of health," does not serve the same purpose as milk. Consuming a small quantity of yogurt as part of a meal activates digestion. Not only does it fully digest in the system within an hour, it also helps the body to assimilate the vitamins and minerals from other foods. With protein, calcium, magnesium, riboflavin, vitamins B6 and B12, and more, it is an ideal food that should be consumed with every meal. It helps to destroy harmful bacteria and encourages "healthy bacteria," which strenghten the digestive system. Yogurt should be plain, organic, and low-fat or nonfat because the imitations of natural yogurt are loaded with fillers, gels, and other foreign ingredients that destroy the real benefits of yogurt. Yoga recommends the daily use of yogurt in Chaach (Yogurt Chaach Cooler, page 32), which should be consumed instead of water with every meal.

Traditional Preparation

It is easy to prepare yogurt at home: Heat 5 to 6 cups of natural or organic milk and bring to a boil. Set it aside to cool. Add 1 tablespoon organic yogurt, cover, and store overnight in a warm place. The result is homemade natural yogurt in the morning. Refrigerate and use within 3 to 4 days. Keep 1 tablespoon aside to repeat the process for making the next batch of yogurt, using the same yogurt culture.

COTTAGE CHEESE (PANEER)

Cottage cheese is a fresh cheese, that is, one that is not aged. It is not a fermented milk product, so it cannot be ripened like other cheeses, as boiling is known to destroy all the organisms. Since aging techniques run contrary to the Sattvic benefits of milk, cottage cheese is a recommended part of the yogic diet. Paneer can be eaten by itself or cooked with other vegetables. This cheese is of high nutritional value due to its high concentration of proteins.

Traditional Preparation

Paneer, the yogic cheese, is prepared at home by adding a few drops of lemon juice to boiling milk (organic and low-fat), then straining it through a muslin cloth. Let the contents hang in the muslin cloth for 30 minutes, to remove as much moisture as possible. After straining, weigh the contents of the cloth down by placing a heavy object over the cloth and leave for 1 hour. The paneer is now ready to use either crumbled or cubed. Alternatively, use low-fat or nonfat organic cottage cheese, available in grocery stores.

drinks

YOGURT CHAACH COOLER

ORANGE BEET BLOSSOM

GINGER-LEMON CRUSH

COOL CUCUMBER MYSTIQUE

PAPAYA-PINEAPPLE FEST

MANGO PANNA

ALMOND AND PISTACHIO MILK SHAKE

FRUIT AND NUT MEDLEY

VEGGIE INFUSION

STRAWBERRY LASSI

yogurt chaach cooler {Sattvic}

SERVES 2 ❧ *Preparation time: 5 minutes*

INGREDIENTS

1 cup nonfat plain yogurt

2 pinches of roasted cumin powder

Salt to taste

1 sprig mint, stems removed and
    leaves finely chopped

METHOD

1. In a medium bowl with a pouring spout, whisk together the yogurt and 4 cups water.

2. Add the roasted cumin powder and salt; stir until blended.

3. Pour the mixture into two glasses and garnish each with chopped mint leaves. The consistency of the chaach should be very thin and watery.

NOTE Chaach can be consumed on a daily basis and is an ideal substitute for water, either with or at the end of a meal. It is a cooling drink, unique for its digestive properties and health benefits.

Om Chant I

Did You Know? Yogurt has innumerable health benefits and the ability to prevent several diseases. It is considered to be one of the best sources of calcium and is rich in potassium, protein, and B vitamins, including B12. It also contains lactase, which makes it much easier to digest than milk.

orange beet blossom {Sattvic}

SERVES 2 ❧ *Preparation time: 25 minutes*

INGREDIENTS

½ medium beet

2 oranges

4 slices fresh pineapple

1 tablespoon fresh lime juice

METHOD

1. Place the beet half in a small pan with just enough water to cover it and boil for 10 to 12 minutes, until the beet is tender. When the beet is cool enough to handle, peel and chop it into small pieces.
2. Squeeze the oranges.
3. Combine the pineapple slices, lime juice, orange juice, and chopped beet in a blender or juicer. Blend until smooth and serve immediately.

Om Chant II

Did You Know?   Oranges contain vitamin C (also found in pineapple and lime), which helps to build up immunity against colds.

ginger-lemon crush {Sattvic}

SERVES 2 ❖ *Preparation time: 10 minutes*

INGREDIENTS

Juice of 1 lemon

One ½-inch piece of ginger, peeled
    and crushed

2 tablespoons honey

Pinch of salt

Ice, crushed or cubed

METHOD

1. Combine the lemon juice, ginger, and 2 cups water in a blender and blend until smooth. Strain the mixture into a bowl or pitcher.
2. Add the honey and a pinch of salt and stir well.
3. Pour the ginger-lemon crush into ice-filled glasses. Serve immediately.

Did You Know? Ginger has antiviral, antifungal, antihistaminic, and antibacterial properties. It's basically the natural version of what you're getting when you take antibiotics, cold and flu tablets, and cough mixtures.

Sukh Asana
(Easy Pose)

cool cucumber mystique {Sattvic}

SERVES 2 ❖ *Preparation time: 10 minutes*

INGREDIENTS

1 small cucumber

1 cup nonfat plain yogurt

½ cup soy milk

2 pinches of roasted cumin powder

Pinch of black pepper

Salt to taste

Leaves from 1 sprig mint

METHOD

1. Peel and grate the cucumber; set aside.

2. Combine the yogurt, soy milk, and 2 cups water in a blender; blend until smooth.

3. Add the cumin, pepper, and salt to the yogurt mixture; blend until combined.

4. Add the grated cucumber and mix well.

5. Garnish with mint leaves and serve immediately.

Did You Know? Cucumber is very cooling for the body and contains vitamins A and C, calcium, and iron. Soy milk is also high in protein and calcium.

Sthith-Prarthana Asana
(Standing Prayer Pose)

papaya-pineapple fest {Sattvic}

SERVES 2 ❖ *Preparation time: 10 minutes*

INGREDIENTS

2 slices papaya, peeled and cubed

2 slices pineapple

½ banana

2 cups nonfat milk

2 tablespoons honey

Pinch of cardamom powder

METHOD

1. In a blender, combine the papaya, pineapple, banana, milk, and ½ cup water; blend until smooth.

2. Add the honey and cardamon powder and stir until well combined. Serve immediately.

Yoni Mudra
(Yogic Seal)

Did You Know? Papaya aids digestion and helps to relieve heartburn because the enzymes of the fruit help to break down proteins, fats, and starches. It contains antioxidant properties, along with beta-carotene and vitamin C. Minerals found in papaya include potassium, magnesium, and calcium.

mango panna {Sattvic}

SERVES 2 ❧ *Preparation time: 30 minutes, plus chilling time*

INGREDIENTS

1 medium unripe mango

One ½-inch piece of ginger,
   peeled and crushed

¼ cup organic sugar

1 teaspoon roasted cumin powder

Pinch of black pepper

Salt to taste

Ice, crushed

Leaves from 1 sprig mint, crushed

METHOD

1. Place the whole mango in a saucepan, add 4 cups water, and bring to a simmer. Cook for about 15 minutes, until the mango is soft. Drain and allow to cool.

2. Peel the mango, remove and discard the seed, and place the pulp in a blender or food processor. Add ½ cup water and blend until smooth.

3. Add the ginger, sugar, cumin, pepper, and salt to the mango pulp. Add 3½ cups water to the mixture and blend until the panna is thin and smooth.

4. Place the panna in the refrigerator to chill for at least 2 hours.

5. Serve the chilled panna over ice, garnished with mint leaves.

Ardh-Padma Asana
(Half-Lotus Pose)

Did You Know? Unripe mango is an excellent source of vitamin C and a rich source of pectin. It is tart in taste and yields a thirst-quenching juice that is ideal for the summer months.

almond and pistachio milk shake {Sattvic}

SERVES 2 ❖ *Preparation time: 10 minutes*

INGREDIENTS

4–6 almonds, blanched if possible

10–12 shelled green pistachios

1 teaspoon cardamom powder

Small pinch of saffron threads

2 cups soy milk or nonfat milk

1 tablespoon honey

METHOD

1. If you do not have blanched almonds, immerse the almonds in boiling water very briefly—just until the skins pucker—then remove them from the water and peel off the skins. Alternatively, soak them for 45 minutes in cool water, then remove the skins. Allow the nuts to dry.

2. In a blender, grind the almonds, pistachios, cardamom, and saffron until combined.

3. Add the milk and honey to the nut mixture and blend until smooth. Serve chilled.

Did You Know? Pistachios contain potassium, phosphorus, and magnesium salts. They are high in fat and protein and are known to help control hypertension and to improve mental energy.

Yoga Mudra
(Symbol of Yoga)

fruit and nut medley {Sattvic}

SERVES 2 ❧ *Preparation time: 10 minutes*

INGREDIENTS

½ medium apple, peeled, cored, and cubed

2 slices pineapple

2 figs, soaked in water for 3 to 4 hours

1 tablespoon honey

4–5 cashews, finely chopped

METHOD

1. Combine the apple, pineapple, figs, and 3 cups water in a blender; blend until smooth.
2. Add the honey and chopped cashews and stir well. Serve immediately.

Garud Asana
(Eagle Pose)

Did You Know? Fruits are full of vitamins, minerals, antioxidants, and fiber, and they are known to reduce the risk of serious diseases. It is best to consume them raw and uncooked—and at peak ripeness—to reap the full benefit of their nutrients and help the body rejuvenate.

veggie infusion {Sattvic}

SERVES 2 ❖ *Preparation time: 10 minutes*

INGREDIENTS

1 tomato, diced

¼ cup chopped green cabbage

1 cup peeled and diced carrot

8–10 spinach leaves, stems removed, chopped

Pinch of black pepper

Salt to taste

Leaves from 1 sprig mint, crushed

METHOD

1. Combine the tomato, cabbage, carrot, spinach, and 1 cup water in a blender or food processor; puree until smooth. Strain the mixture through a sieve.

2. Add the pepper and salt.

3. Garnish with mint leaves and serve.

NOTE With the Veggie Infusion, a little bit goes a long way. It is intended to be consumed in small portions of 1 cup or less.

Did You Know? All vegetables contain some of the vitamins and minerals that are necessary to maintain a healthy immune system, as well as dietary fiber. It is recommended that you include a generous variety of vegetables in your daily food plan. Try to consume at least four servings daily.

Tal Asana I
(Tree Pose I)

strawberry lassi {Sattvic}

SERVES 2 ❖ *Preparation time: 10 minutes, plus chilling time*

INGREDIENTS

½ cup strawberries, washed and
    hulled
¼ cup raspberries
1 cup low-fat plain yogurt
1 tablespoon organic sugar

METHOD

1. Combine all the ingredients and 2 cups water in a blender; blend until smooth.
2. Chill for at least 1 hour and serve.

Tal Asana II
(Tree Pose II)

Did You Know? Strawberries are loaded with vitamin C and antioxidants, which are thought to help protect against cancer. Raspberries, too, contain lots of vitamin C, as well as vitamin E, folate, and potassium. Both berries have very few calories and are good sources of fiber.

soups and salads

TOMATO, CARROT, AND CABBAGE SOUP

GREEN PEA SOUP

BEET SOUP

LENTIL-SPINACH SOUP

ROASTED PUMPKIN SOUP

BARLEY VEGETABLE SOUP

BEAN SPROUT SALAD

SESAME TOFU AND CARROT SALAD

FRUIT AND VEGETABLE SALAD

CORN, TOMATO, AND CUCUMBER SALAD

ASPARAGUS-MUSHROOM SALAD

LEAFY SALAD

tomato, carrot, and cabbage soup {Sattvic}

SERVES 2–3 ❖ *Preparation time: 55 minutes*

INGREDIENTS

2 tomatoes

1 carrot, peeled and diced

1 potato, peeled and diced

1 tablespoon olive oil

1 cup cabbage, grated or finely
    chopped

Salt to taste

Leaves from 1 sprig cilantro

METHOD

1. Place the whole tomatoes in a small saucepan. Add 2 to 3 cups water (enough to cover) and bring to a boil. Reduce the heat and simmer for 10 to 12 minutes, until soft. Drain, reserving ½ cup of the cooking liquid. Set the tomatoes aside to cool.

2. When the tomatoes are cool enough to handle, remove and discard the skins and seeds. Place the tomatoes in a blender or food processor with the reserved cooking liquid and puree until smooth. Transfer the puree to a bowl.

3. Place the carrot and potato in a small saucepan. Add 1½ cups water and bring to a boil. Reduce the heat and simmer for about 20 minutes, until soft. Transfer the contents of the pot to a blender or food processor; puree until smooth.

4. Heat the olive oil in a stockpot over medium heat. Add the cabbage and cook, stirring occasionally, for 5 minutes, or until partially tender.

5. Add the pureed vegetables, 2 cups water, and salt and simmer for 10 minutes.

6. Ladle into soup bowls, garnish with cilantro leaves, and serve.

Gomukh Asana
(Cow Face Pose)

Did You Know? Tomatoes are naturally low in fat and calories, high in fiber and vitamins, and rich in health-promoting plant chemicals, such as lycopene, which is believed to be protective against cancer and heart disease.

green pea soup {Sattvic}

SERVES 2 ❧ *Preparation time: 30 minutes*

INGREDIENTS

3 cups fresh, shelled green peas

1 teaspoon ghee or butter

1 tablespoon semolina

1 cup nonfat milk

1 teaspoon roasted cumin powder

Salt to taste

Leaves from 1 sprig parsley, chopped

METHOD

1. Bring a pot of water to a boil and add the green peas. Cook for 8 to 10 minutes, until soft; drain. Set aside ½ cup peas. Mash the remaining peas into a paste or puree them in a blender.

2. In a large saucepan, melt the ghee or butter over medium heat. Stir in the semolina. Add the mashed peas and bring the mixture to a simmer. Add milk and water, if necessary, to obtain the desired consistency.

3. Stir in the reserved whole peas. Add the cumin and salt.

4. Remove the pan from the heat, pour the soup into bowls, and garnish with parsley before serving.

Parvat Asana I
(Seated Mountain Pose I)

Did You Know? Peas are rich in protein and carbohydrates, low in fats, and a good source of vitamins A, C, and B9 (folic acid) as well as dietary fiber and iron. They are among those vegetables richest in thiamine (also known as vitamin B1), which is essential to energy production, nerve function, and carbohydrate metabolism.

beet soup {Sattvic}

SERVES 2 ❖ *Preparation time: 40 minutes*

INGREDIENTS

1 beet, peeled and julienned
    (cut into matchstick-size pieces)
1 tablespoon olive oil
2 scallions, finely chopped
Salt to taste
2 tablespoons low-fat or nonfat
    plain yogurt
1 teaspoon chopped chives
OPTIONAL—*Rajasic variation:*
1 clove garlic, crushed

METHOD

1. Bring 3 cups water to a boil in a medium saucepan. Add the beets and cook for 10 minutes, or until tender.
2. Meanwhile, heat the olive oil in a large skillet over medium heat for 1 minute. Add the scallions. For the Rajasic variation, also add the garlic. Sauté for 1 minute, until partially tender.
3. Add the beets to the skillet, along with their cooking liquid, and salt to taste. Simmer, stirring occasionally, for 20 minutes.
4. Ladle the soup into bowls and top each with a generous spoonful of yogurt and a sprinkle of chives. Serve hot.

Did You Know?   Beets contain no fat and very few calories and are a great source of fiber.

Padma Asana
(Lotus Pose)

lentil-spinach soup {Sattvic}

SERVES 2 ❖ *Preparation time: 50 minutes*

INGREDIENTS

½ cup yellow moong lentils

1 tablespoon vegetable or olive oil

2 teaspoons cumin seeds

One 1-inch piece of ginger, peeled
    and crushed

1 stalk celery, finely chopped

2 scallions, finely chopped

8–10 large leaves spinach, chopped

2 pinches of turmeric powder

Salt to taste

1 tablespoon lemon juice

METHOD

1. Combine the lentils and 4 cups water in a medium saucepan; soak for 10 to 15 minutes. Bring to a boil over high heat. Reduce the heat and simmer for about 25 minutes, until the lentils are tender.

2. Heat the oil in a soup pot over medium heat for 1 minute. Add the cumin seeds. When the seeds start to splutter, add the ginger, celery, and scallions. Cook for 2 minutes.

3. Add the spinach and cook for about 5 minutes, until wilted.

4. Pour the lentils, along with their cooking liquid, into the soup pot. Add the turmeric and salt to taste. Reduce the heat and simmer for 2 minutes.

5. Add lemon juice and serve.

Did You Know?   Lentils are packed with nutrients, fiber, and complex carbohydrates, and are a low-calorie, low-fat, and cholesterol-free food. They provide more folic acid (vitamin B9) than any other unfortified food. (Folic acid is a vitamin that is essential for growth and good health. The body cannot make it, so it must be obtained from foods and supplements.)

Ekpad Asana
(One-Leg Pose)

roasted pumpkin soup {Sattvic}

SERVES 2–3 ❖ *Preparation time: 50 minutes*

INGREDIENTS

One 1-pound pumpkin, peeled,
    seeded, and cut into chunks
1 tablespoon olive oil
1 potato, peeled and chopped
1 carrot, peeled and chopped
One 1-inch piece of ginger, peeled
    and finely chopped
1 stalk celery, chopped
1 teaspoon cumin powder
Salt to taste
½ cup sour cream
1 sprig parsley, finely chopped

METHOD

1. Preheat the oven to 350°F. Grease a baking sheet and arrange the pumpkin chunks in a single layer. Lightly brush the pumpkin with half of the olive oil. Bake for 25 minutes, until slightly brown around the edges.

2. Meanwhile, bring a pot of water to a boil. Add the potato and carrot and cook for about 15 minutes, until tender. With a slotted spoon or strainer, remove the vegetables from the cooking liquid. Set the liquid aside for the stock.

3. Heat the remaining oil in a large pot. Add the ginger, celery, and cumin. Cook, stirring occasionally, for 3 minutes.

4. Add the cooked potato and carrot, roasted pumpkin, and reserved cooking liquid and bring the soup to a boil. Reduce the heat and simmer for 15 minutes.

5. Remove the pot from the heat and set the soup aside to cool.

6. When the soup has cooled to room temperature, transfer it to a blender and puree it until smooth. Season with salt.

7. Ladle the soup into bowls, top each serving with a spoonful of sour cream and a sprinkling of parsley, and serve.

Utkat Asana
(Powerful Pose)

Did You Know? Pumpkins are a source of vitamins and minerals, particularly beta-carotene, vitamin C, and potassium.

barley vegetable soup {Sattvic}

SERVES 2–3 ❖ *Preparation time: 20 minutes*

INGREDIENTS

1 tablespoon olive oil

1 carrot, peeled and grated or finely chopped

½ cup grated or finely chopped cabbage

8–10 French beans, cut lengthwise into thin strips

½ cup barley, boiled

Salt to taste

Black pepper to taste

METHOD

1. Heat the olive oil in a medium pot over medium heat for 1 minute. Add the carrot, cabbage, and beans and cook, stirring occasionally, for 5 minutes, or until partially tender.
2. Add the barley, 6 cups water, and salt to taste and bring to a boil. Reduce the heat and cook for 10 minutes.
3. Ladle the soup into bowls, sprinkle each with black pepper, and serve.

Did You Know? Barley, an overall health protector, contains most of the vitamins, minerals, and proteins required by the body that are easily assimilated through the digestive tract. It has been found to lower total cholesterol levels and improve several cardiovascular risk factors.

Trikon Asana Variation
(Triangle Pose Variation)

bean sprout salad {Sattvic}

SERVES 2 ❧ *Preparation time: 35 minutes*

INGREDIENTS

2 teaspoons vegetable or olive oil

1 teaspoon mustard seeds

1 cup moth beans (or green moong
    lentils), sprouted

Pinch of turmeric powder

Salt to taste

1 teaspoon lemon juice

1 sprig cilantro, finely chopped

METHOD

1. Heat the oil in a large saucepan over medium heat for
   1 minute and add the mustard seeds. When the seeds start
   to splutter, stir in the bean sprouts. Add ½ cup of water
   and stir.

2. Cover the pan, reduce the heat to low, and cook, stirring
   occasionally, for 25 to 30 minutes, or until the bean
   sprouts are soft.

3. Add the turmeric and salt and continue cooking for
   5 minutes.

4. Remove the pan from the heat and stir in the lemon juice.

5. Sprinkle the bean sprouts with cilantro and serve warm.

NOTE To sprout beans: Place the moth beans or lentils in a bowl with enough
water to cover and soak them, covered, for 6 to 7 hours. Drain the beans dry and
cover them with a lid. Let sit overnight in a warm place to enable the seeds to
germinate and form sprouts.

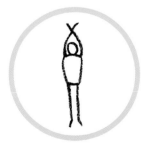

Tal Asana III
(Tree Pose III)

Did You Know? Bean sprouts contain as much vitamin A as a lemon,
thiamine (vitamin B1) equal to that of an avocado, the same amount of carbohydrate as a melon, and niacin equal to that of a banana! With their high
levels of concentrated plant compounds, sprouts can protect against disease.

sesame tofu and carrot salad {Sattvic}

SERVES 2 ❖ *Preparation time: 30 minutes*

INGREDIENTS

1 tablespoon sesame oil

1 pound firm tofu, cut into bite-size
    triangles

1 scallion, finely sliced

One 1-inch piece of ginger, peeled
    and grated

1 teaspoon roasted cumin powder

2 tablespoons soy sauce

¼ cup finely shredded cabbage

1 cucumber, peeled and cut into
    paper-thin ribbons with a peeler

2 carrots, peeled and cut into paper-
    thin ribbons with a peeler

1 teaspoon honey

1 tablespoon lime juice

2 tablespoons roasted peanuts

Leaves from 1 sprig mint, finely
    chopped

METHOD

1   Heat the sesame oil in a nonstick frying pan over medium heat for 1 minute. Add the tofu, scallion, ginger, cumin, and soy sauce. Cook, stirring occasionally, for 2 to 3 minutes, until the tofu is golden. Remove the pan from the heat and allow the mixture to cool.

2. Arrange the cabbage on a large platter, top it with the cucumber and carrots, and spoon the tofu over them.

3. Whisk the honey and lime juice together in a small bowl and drizzle the mixture over the salad.

4. Sprinkle the salad with peanuts and mint leaves and serve.

Did You Know? Tofu, a soybean product, is high in protein and calcium, low in saturated fat and salt, and cholesterol-free.

Kon Asana I
(Angle Pose I)

fruit and vegetable salad {Sattvic}

SERVES 2–3 ❖ *Preparation time: 25–30 minutes*

INGREDIENTS

½ potato, diced

½ carrot, peeled and diced

¼ cup French beans, finely chopped

½ apple, cored and cut into small cubes

2 pineapple slices, cut into small chunks

½ cup grapes, halved

1½ cups nonfat plain yogurt

¼ cup honey

Pinch of salt

1 tablespoon chopped almonds

8–10 raisins

METHOD

1. In a vegetable steamer or a sieve set inside a pot, steam the potato, carrot, and French beans together for about 15 minutes, or until tender. Set aside to cool.

2. In a serving bowl, combine the cooled steamed vegetables with the apple, pineapple, and grapes.

3. For the dressing, whisk the yogurt, honey, and salt in a small bowl until blended.

4. Add the dressing to the salad and toss well to combine. Sprinkle the salad with almonds and raisins and serve.

Did You Know? A diet high in fruits and vegetables helps prevent and cure a wide range of ailments. The more you eat, the better. Fruits and vegetables contain phytochemicals, which are known to help fight some of the most deadly diseases. Fresh vegetables (with the exception of avocados and olives) are fat-, cholesterol-, and sodium-free and have few calories. They are much, much more than fiber and water: Vegetables are the most fiber-rich, nutrient-packed foods in the diet.

Kon Asana II
(Angle Pose II)

corn, tomato, and cucumber salad {Sattvic}

SERVES 2 ❖ *Preparation time: 20 minutes*

INGREDIENTS

1 ear corn

2 teaspoons sesame oil

1 teaspoon mustard seeds

1 tomato, finely chopped

1 cucumber, peeled and finely
    chopped

1 teaspoon roasted cumin powder

Pinch of sugar

Salt to taste

1 sprig cilantro, finely chopped

METHOD

1. Using a sharp knife, cut all the corn kernels off the cob.

2. Heat the oil in a large saucepan over medium heat for 1 minute, then add the mustard seeds. When the seeds start to splutter, add the corn and cook, covered, over low heat, stirring occasionally, for 10 minutes, or until the corn is soft. Remove the pan from the heat and let cool. Transfer the corn to a serving bowl.

3. Add the chopped tomato and cucumber to the bowl. Stir in the cumin, sugar, and salt. Sprinkle with chopped cilantro and serve at room temperature.

Did You Know?   Sesame oil, oil pressed from sesame seeds, is one of those vegetable oils that is good for you. It is rich in mono- and poly-unsaturated fats—the good type of fat that cuts cholesterol—and low in saturated fats—the fat that's bad for you. It also contains powerful antioxidants called sesamol and sesamin.

Kon Asana III
(Angle Pose III)

asparagus-mushroom salad {Rajasic}

SERVES 2 ❖ *Preparation time: 10 minutes*

INGREDIENTS

4 asparagus spears, halved diagonally

2 tablespoons olive oil

1 teaspoon mustard seeds

1 red bell pepper, cut into strips

½ cup (about ¼ pound) button
     mushrooms, halved

¼ cup orange juice

2 tablespoons lime juice

2 teaspoons lemon juice

¼ cup honey

METHOD

1. Bring 1 cup water to a boil in a small skillet. Add the asparagus and cook for 1 to 2 minutes, until just tender; drain. Plunge the asparagus into cold water to stop the cooking.

2. Heat the oil in a large saucepan over medium heat for 1 minute and add the mustard seeds. When the mustard seeds start to splutter, add the bell pepper and mushrooms.

3. Reduce the heat and add the orange, lime, and lemon juices and the honey. Stir for 2 minutes, remove from the heat, and allow to cool.

4. Add the asparagus to the mushroom mixture and toss to combine. Serve.

Chakra Asana Variation
(Wheel Pose Variation)

Did You Know? Mushrooms are low in calories, have no cholesterol, and are virtually free of fat and sodium. They contain some of the essential minerals and B-complex vitamins not easily found in produce.

leafy salad {Sattvic}

SERVES 2 ❖ *Preparation time: 10 minutes*

INGREDIENTS

2 cups chopped spinach leaves

1 cup chopped lettuce leaves

¼ cup diced fresh pineapple

½ cup cottage cheese

1 tablespoon honey

2 teaspoons lemon juice

Salt to taste

METHOD

1. In a salad bowl, toss the spinach, lettuce, pineapple, and cottage cheese together.

2. For the dressing, whisk the honey, lemon juice, and salt in a small bowl until blended.

3. Add the dressing to the greens and toss to combine. Serve.

Did You Know? Leafy greens supply many of the vitamins and minerals we need to stay healthy and fit. They are a rich source of vitamins A, C, and folate. They possess antioxidants and phytochemicals, thought to be strong disease fighters. Eating leafy greens may help maintain eye health, reduce the risk of some cancers, and keep bones and teeth strong.

Ardha Matsya Asana
(Fish Pose)

raita and chutney

apple-pineapple raita {Sattvic}

SERVES 4 ❖ *Preparation time: 10 minutes*

INGREDIENTS

3 cups low-fat or nonfat plain yogurt

¼ cup nonfat milk

1 apple, peeled, cored, and diced

4 slices pineapple, peeled and diced

2 tablespoons honey

Pinch of cardamom powder

10–15 raisins

METHOD

1. Whisk the yogurt, nonfat milk, and ½ cup water in a medium bowl until blended.

2. Stir in the diced apple and pineapple. Add the honey and cardamom.

3. Garnish with raisins and serve.

Did You Know? Pineapple is rich in folate and is an excellent source of vitamin C. Pineapples are also nutritionally high in the enzyme bromelain, which aids digestion by breaking down the amino-acid bonds in proteins.

Hastpad Asana
(Hands to Feet Pose)

vegetable raita {Sattvic}

SERVES 4 ❧ *Preparation time: 20 minutes*

INGREDIENTS

3 cups nonfat plain yogurt

1 cucumber, finely chopped

1 tomato, finely chopped

1 green bell pepper, finely chopped

1 teaspoon roasted cumin powder

Salt to taste

2 teaspoons vegetable or olive oil

Pinch of asafetida

1 teaspoon mustard seeds

1 sprig cilantro, finely chopped
(leaves and stems)

METHOD

1. Whisk the yogurt and ½ cup water in a medium bowl until blended. Add the chopped cucumber, tomato, and bell pepper, then stir in the cumin and salt.

2. Heat the oil in a small saucepan over medium heat for 1 minute. Add the asafetida and mustard seeds. When the mustard seeds start to splutter, remove the pan from the heat and allow it to cool.

3. Add the mustard seeds to the yogurt mixture, sprinkle with cilantro, and serve.

Vakra Asana II
(Twist Posture II)

Did You Know? For maximum nutrient retention, vegetables should be eaten raw. Vitamins and minerals found in certain raw vegetables are known to have anticancer, antioxidant, and hormone-enhancing properties.

pomegranate and spinach raita {Sattvic}

SERVES 4 ❖ *Preparation time: 20 minutes*

INGREDIENTS

3 cups nonfat plain yogurt

1 cup finely chopped spinach

Seeds from 1 pomegranate

1 teaspoon roasted cumin powder

Pinch of black pepper

1 teaspoon organic sugar

Salt to taste

METHOD

1. Whisk the yogurt and ½ cup water in a medium bowl until blended.

2. Combine the spinach and ½ cup water in a small saucepan. Cook over low heat for 3 to 4 minutes. Drain the spinach and allow it to cool.

3. Add the wilted spinach and pomegranate seeds to the yogurt mixture and stir well.

4. Stir in the cumin, pepper, sugar, and salt and serve.

Did You Know? Pomegranate is one of the best sources of anti-oxidants. One pomegranate provides most of the body's daily potassium and vitamin C needs and a healthy dose of fiber.

Parvat Asana II
(Seated Mountain Pose II)

avocado-tomato raita {Sattvic}

SERVES 4 ❖ *Preparation time: 15 minutes*

INGREDIENTS

3 cups nonfat plain yogurt

1 tomato, diced

1 avocado, peeled, pitted, and diced

1 teaspoon roasted cumin powder

Salt to taste

1 sprig cilantro, chopped

OPTIONAL—*Rajasic variation:*

1 teaspoon finely chopped garlic

1 small jalapeño or green pepper,
   chopped

METHOD

1. Whisk the yogurt and ½ cup water in a medium bowl until blended. Stir in the diced tomato and avocado. Add the cumin and salt. For the Rajasic variation, also add the garlic and jalapeño.
2. Garnish with cilantro and serve.

Bhadra Asana
(Throne Pose)

Did You Know? Avocado is rich in flavor and is a good source of phytochemicals. It has larger amounts of vitamin E than most fruits, and more pantothenic acid—a water-soluble vitamin considered by many to relieve stress.

cilantro-mint chutney {Sattvic}

SERVES 6 ❖ *Preparation time: 15 minutes*

INGREDIENTS

1 cup chopped cilantro

Leaves from 1 sprig mint, chopped

One 1-inch piece of ginger, peeled
and finely chopped

1 tablespoon grated coconut

1 teaspoon lime juice

1 teaspoon cumin seeds

Pinch of organic sugar

Salt to taste

OPTIONAL—Rajasic variation:

1 teaspoon finely chopped garlic

1 small green chili, chopped

METHOD

1. Combine the cilantro, mint, ginger, coconut, and lime
   juice in a small bowl. For the Rajasic variation, also add
   the garlic and chili. Stir in the cumin seeds, sugar, and salt.
2. Pour the mixture into a blender, add ¼ cup water, and
   blend until smooth. Serve.

Did You Know? Cilantro contains chemicals and compounds that fight allergies. It is known to improve digestion and has strong anti-inflammatory effects.

Parvat Asana III
(Seated Mountain Pose III)

tomato-cheese dip {Sattvic}

SERVES 4–6 ❖ *Preparation time: 15 minutes*

INGREDIENTS

1 teaspoon olive oil

1 large tomato, chopped

1 scallion, finely chopped

One ½-inch piece of ginger, peeled
and finely chopped

1 teaspoon roasted cumin powder

Pinch of organic sugar

Salt to taste

½ cup low-fat ricotta or cottage
cheese

OPTIONAL—Rajasic variation:

1 teaspoon finely chopped garlic

1 small green chili, chopped

Pinch of red chili powder

METHOD

1. In a small skillet, heat the olive oil over medium heat for 1 minute. Add the tomato, scallion, and ginger. For the Rajasic variation, also add the garlic and green chili. Sauté for 2 to 3 minutes, or until tender.

2. Add the cumin, sugar, and salt. For the Rajasic variation, also add the red chili powder.

3. Add the ricotta or cottage cheese, stirring until well combined, and serve.

Did You Know? Scallion is a low-calorie, low-sodium, cholesterol-free vegetable and is known to protect against serious illnesses such as cancer, while lowering blood pressure and cholesterol.

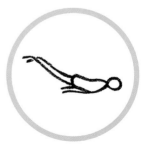

Shalabh Asana
(Locust Pose)

green dip {Sattvic}

SERVES 4–6 ❖ *Preparation time: 15 minutes*

INGREDIENTS

¼ cup chopped cilantro leaves

¼ cup chopped parsley leaves

1 small green bell pepper, chopped

3 cups nonfat plain yogurt

Salt to taste

Black pepper to taste

METHOD

1. Combine the cilantro, parsley, and bell pepper in a blender and blend well.

2. In a medium bowl, whip the yogurt until it thickens. Stir in the herb mixture. Season with salt and pepper and serve.

Yastik Asana
(Stick Pose)

Did You Know? Parsley is high in vitamins C and B12 and beta-carotene. It is good for the heart, stomach, and blood pressure, and can help relieve some arthritis aches and pains. It is also used to treat urinary tract infections, control indigestion and gas, and act as a digestive aid.

vegetables and curries

french beans with coconut {Sattvic}

SERVES 2 ❖ *Preparation time: 30 minutes*

INGREDIENTS

2 teaspoons vegetable oil

Pinch of asafetida

1 teaspoon cumin seeds

3–4 curry leaves

1 pound French beans, washed and
quartered lengthwise

½ teaspoon turmeric powder

Salt to taste

½ cup grated fresh coconut

METHOD

1. Heat the oil in a medium skillet over medium heat for
1 minute. Add the asafetida and cumin seeds. When the
seeds start to splutter, add the curry leaves and beans
and sauté for 5 to 8 minutes.

2. Add the turmeric and salt. Cook for 2 to 3 minutes,
until the beans are tender.

4. Stir in the grated coconut, remove the beans from the heat,
and serve.

NOTE Serve with whole-wheat tortilla or roti.

Bhujang Asana
(Cobra Pose)

Did You Know? French beans contain elements that increase the blood's ability to coagulate and help decrease the level of cholesterol in the body.

jaipur peas and baby potatoes {Sattvic}

SERVES 2 ❖ *Preparation time: 30 minutes*

INGREDIENTS

½ cup organic nonfat or low-fat
 plain yogurt

Salt to taste

Pinch of turmeric powder

1 teaspoon roasted cumin powder

1 teaspoon coriander powder

2 teaspoons vegetable oil

Pinch of asafetida

1 teaspoon fennel seeds

One 1-inch piece of ginger, peeled
 and chopped

1 cup or 8 small white baby potatoes,
 peeled and boiled

1 cup fresh, shelled green peas, boiled

1 sprig cilantro, finely chopped

OPTIONAL—Rajasic variation:

Pinch of red chili powder

METHOD

1. Whisk yogurt in a small bowl. Add salt, turmeric, cumin, and coriander; whisk until blended. For the Rajasic variation, also add the red chili powder.

2. Heat the oil in a medium skillet over medium heat for 1 minute. Add the asafetida and fennel seeds. When the seeds start to splutter, add the ginger.

3. Reduce the heat. Slowly add the yogurt and simmer, stirring continuously, for 2 to 3 minutes.

4. Now, add ½ cup of water and continue stirring for 2 minutes (NOTE: This is to prevent the yogurt from curdling.)

5. Add the potatoes and peas and continue cooking, stirring occasionally, for 10 minutes longer.

6. Remove the pan from the heat and transfer to a serving dish.

7. Garnish with cilantro and serve.

NOTES   Make sure to use a clean skillet and homemade or organic yogurt to reduce the risk of curdling. ❖ For a variation on this dish, substitute boiled cauliflower and beans for the potatoes. ❖ Serve with whole-wheat tortilla, roti, or rice.

Did You Know?   Coriander powder, a popular spice, not only enhances the freshness and flavor of any dish, it also helps relieve indigestion. Its seeds are known to reduce high cholesterol.

Dhanur-Vakra Asana
(Bow Pose)

simple okra {Sattvic}

SERVES 2 ❖ *Preparation time: 30 minutes*

INGREDIENTS

2 teaspoons vegetable or olive oil

Pinch of asafetida

1 teaspoon mustard seeds

1 pound okra, washed, patted dry,
    and cut into ¼-inch pieces

1 tablespoon coriander powder

½ teaspoon turmeric powder

Salt to taste

1 teaspoon lemon juice

OPTIONAL—Rajasic variation:

Pinch of red chili powder

METHOD

1. Heat the oil in a medium skillet over medium heat for
   1 minute. Add the asafetida and mustard seeds. When the
   seeds start to splutter, add the okra. Reduce the heat to low,
   cover, and cook for about 10 minutes, until the okra is
   partially done.

2. Add the coriander, turmeric, and salt. For the Rajasic
   variation, also add the red chili powder. Cook, stirring
   occasionally, for 2 to 3 minutes, until the okra is tender.

3. Remove the skillet from the heat and stir in the lemon juice.
   Serve hot.

NOTE Serve with whole-wheat tortilla or roti.

Ardha-Matsyendra Asana
(Half Spinal Twist)

Did You Know? Okra is low-calorie, free of cholesterol and saturated fat, and high in the antioxidant vitamins C, A, and B6. It is a good source of folic acid.

mixed vegetable patties {Sattvic}

SERVES 2–3 ❖ *Preparation time: 45 minutes*

INGREDIENTS

¼ pound (2–3 stalks) broccoli,
    steamed

¼ pound mushrooms, steamed

¼ pound (3–4 florets) cauliflower,
    steamed

½ pound (2 medium) potatoes,
    peeled and boiled

2 teaspoons roasted cumin powder

Salt to taste

2 teaspoons olive oil

½ cup finely chopped scallions
    (both bulbs and green leaves)

METHOD

1. Combine all the cooked vegetables in a large mixing bowl and mash them. Add the cumin and salt; stir to combine.

2. Heat 1 teaspoon of the olive oil in a medium skillet over medium heat for 1 minute. Add the scallions and sauté for 2 minutes.

3. Add the sautéed scallions to the vegetable mixture and stir until thoroughly combined. Using your hands, form the mixture into 8 to 10 medium-size thick patties.

4. Brush a skillet with the remaining teaspoon of olive oil and heat it over medium heat for 1 minute. Arrange the patties in a single layer in the skillet and cook, turning once, for 10 to 15 minutes, until they are heated through. Serve hot.

NOTE   Serve with Cilantro-Mint Chutney (page 69) or Green Dip (page 72).

Did You Know?   Vegetarianism is about more than not eating meat; it's also about smart eating. The American Dietetic Association has proclaimed that "appropriately planned vegetarian diets are healthful, nutritionally adequate, and provide health benefits."

Hastpad-Angust Asana I
(Extended Hand to Toe Pose I)

eggplant bharta {Sattvic}

SERVES 2 ❖ *Preparation time: 40 minutes*

INGREDIENTS

1 medium eggplant, halved

2 teaspoons vegetable oil

Pinch of asafetida

1 teaspoon cumin seeds

1 tablespoon peeled and finely
    chopped ginger

1 tomato, finely chopped

1 teaspoon coriander powder

1 teaspoon turmeric powder

Salt to taste

¼ cup low-fat plain yogurt

OPTIONAL—*Rajasic variation:*

1 teaspoon finely chopped garlic

1 small red onion, finely chopped

Pinch of red chili powder

METHOD

1. Preheat the oven to 450°F.

2. Place the eggplant halves, cut side up, on a baking sheet and roast for about 20 minutes, or until the flesh is tender and the skin is slightly burnt. Set aside to cool.

3. When the eggplant is cool enough to handle, spoon the pulp out of the skin and into a medium bowl. Set aside.

4. Heat the oil in a medium skillet over medium heat for 1 minute. Add the asafetida and cumin seeds. When the cumin seeds start to splutter, add the ginger and tomato. For the Rajasic variation, also add the garlic, onion, and red chili powder. Sauté for 1 minute.

5. Add the coriander, turmeric, and salt and cook for 2 minutes longer.

6. Add the eggplant pulp and yogurt and stir well. Cook, stirring occasionally, for 10 minutes, then serve immediately.

NOTE   Serve with whole-wheat tortilla or roti.

Did You Know?   Eggplant may lower blood cholesterol and help counteract some of the detrimental blood effects of fatty foods. Eggplant also has antibacterial and diuretic properties.

Hastpad-Angust Asana III
(Extended Hand to Toe Pose III)

potato subzi {Sattvic}

SERVES 2 ❖ *Preparation time: 30 minutes*

INGREDIENTS

2 tablespoons oil

Pinch of asafetida

1 teaspoon mustard seeds

1 teaspoon fennel seeds

2–3 curry leaves

One ½-inch piece of ginger, peeled
and finely chopped

1 large potato, peeled and cut into
medium chunks

1 tablespoon coriander powder

½ teaspoon turmeric powder

1 teaspoon roasted cumin powder

Salt to taste

1 teaspoon lemon juice

OPTIONAL—Rajasic variation:

1 small green chili, finely chopped

1 red onion, coarsely chopped

Pinch of red chili powder

METHOD

1. Heat the oil in a large saucepan over medium heat for
   1 minute. Add the asafetida, mustard seeds, and fennel seeds.
   When the seeds start to splutter, add the curry leaves and
   ginger. For the Rajasic variation, also add the green chili.

2. Add the potato and cover the pan. Reduce the heat to low
   and cook for about 10 minutes, until the potato chunks are
   partially cooked. For the Rajasic variation, add the onion,
   increase the heat to medium, and sauté for about 5 minutes,
   until the onion is softened.

3. Add the coriander, turmeric, cumin, and salt. For the
   Rajasic version, also add the red chili powder. Cook for
   5 minutes, or until the potato is tender.

4. Remove the pan from the heat. Add the lemon juice and
   serve immediately.

NOTE Serve with whole-wheat tortilla or roti.

Did You Know? Potatoes are saturated-fat free, sodium-free,
cholesterol-free, high in antioxidant vitamin C, and a good source of fiber.
They contain large amounts of potassium, which is believed to be important
for maintaining health and preventing degenerative disease.

Hastpad-Angust Asana II
(Extended Hand to Toe Pose II)

stuffed peppers {Sattvic}

SERVES 2 ❖ *Preparation time: 30 minutes*

INGREDIENTS

2 medium red bell peppers

2 potatoes, about 5 ounces each,
    peeled, boiled, and mashed

1 teaspoon lime juice

½ teaspoon turmeric powder

Salt to taste

2 teaspoons oil

Pinch of asafetida

1 teaspoon fennel seeds

OPTIONAL—*Rajasic variation:*

Pinch of red chili powder

METHOD

1. Slice a small piece off the top of each pepper and remove the seeds and white membranes.

2. Place the mashed potatoes in a medium bowl. Add the lime juice, turmeric, and salt. For the Rajasic variation, also add the red chili powder. Mix well. Spoon the potato mixture into the prepared peppers until they are nearly full.

3. Heat the oil in a deep sauté pan over medium heat for 1 minute. Add the asafetida and fennel seeds. When the seeds start to splutter, place the stuffed peppers, top side up, in the pan. Reduce the heat to low. Cover the pan and cook for 10 minutes.

4. Carefully turn the peppers upside down, without allowing the stuffing to fall out. (NOTE: Some fennel seeds should cling to the stuffing.) Continue to cook over low heat for 5 to 8 minutes longer.

5. Turn the peppers top side up. Test each pepper for doneness by gently pushing against the side. When the pepper is fully cooked, it will feel soft.

6. When the peppers are done, remove the pan from the heat and allow the peppers to cool slightly before serving.

NOTE   Serve with whole-wheat tortilla or roti.

Did You Know?   Brightly colored vegetables like red bell peppers are excellent sources of vitamins C and A, powerful antioxidants with anti-inflammatory properties.

Hastpad-Angust Asana IV
(Extended Hand to Toe Pose IV)

cabbage-carrot mix {Sattvic}

SERVES 2 ❧ *Preparation time: 20 minutes*

INGREDIENTS

I teaspoon oil

I teaspoon mustard seeds

2 cups finely grated cabbage

I cup julienned (cut into matchstick-
    size pieces) carrot

Pinch of turmeric powder

½ teaspoon roasted cumin powder

Salt to taste

I teaspoon lemon juice

METHOD

1. Heat the oil in a medium skillet over medium heat for
   I minute. Add the mustard seeds. When the seeds start
   to splutter, add the cabbage and carrot. Cook, stirring
   occasionally, for 8 to IO minutes.

2. Stir in the turmeric, cumin, and salt.

3. When the carrot and cabbage have softened, remove the
   pan from the heat and add the lemon juice. Serve hot.

NOTE   Serve with whole-wheat tortilla or roti.

Parvat Asana IV
(Seated Mountain Pose IV)

Did You Know?   Cabbage is a source of protein, dietary fiber,
carbohydrates, vitamin C, folate, calcium, and iron. It is also known
to be a cancer fighter.

spinach and cottage cheese {Sattvic}

SERVES 2 ❖ *Preparation time: 45 minutes*

INGREDIENTS

1 pound spinach, thoroughly washed
    and stems discarded
1 teaspoon peeled and finely
    chopped ginger
2 teaspoons oil
Pinch of asafetida
1 teaspoon cumin seeds
1 tomato, finely chopped
1 teaspoon coriander powder
½ teaspoon turmeric powder
Salt to taste
½ cup low-fat cottage cheese
OPTIONAL—Rajasic variation:
1 tablespoon finely chopped garlic
1 small green chili
1 small onion, finely chopped
Pinch of red chili powder

METHOD

1. Bring ½ cup water to a boil in a large saucepan over high heat. Add the spinach leaves. Reduce the heat and cook for 5 to 8 minutes, until the spinach has wilted.

2. Cool and transfer the spinach and the cooking liquid to a blender. Add the ginger. For the Rajasic variation, also add the garlic and green chili. Puree the mixture until smooth. Set the mixture aside.

3. Heat the oil in a medium skillet over medium heat for 1 minute. Add the asafetida and cumin seeds. When the seeds start to splutter, add the tomato. For the Rajasic variation, also add the onion. Cook, stirring occasionally, for 4 to 5 minutes.

4. Stir in the coriander, turmeric, and salt. For the Rajasic variation, also add the red chili powder. Cook for 2 minutes.

5. Add the spinach puree and stir until well combined. Add the cottage cheese and cook, stirring occasionally, for 5 to 8 minutes longer. Serve hot.

NOTE Serve with whole-wheat tortilla or roti.

> **Did You Know?** An excellent source of antioxidants and beta-carotene, spinach is high in lutein and nutrients that help lower blood cholesterol. It also contains carbohydrates, protein, fiber, vitamin A, vitamin C, calcium, iron, and folic acid.

Hams Asana
(Swan Pose)

warm cauliflower {Sattvic}

SERVES 2 ❖ *Preparation time: 30 minutes*

INGREDIENTS

2 teaspoons vegetable oil

Pinch of asafetida

1 teaspoon cumin seeds

One 1-inch piece of ginger, peeled
   and finely chopped

2–3 curry leaves

2 cups cauliflower florets

1 teaspoon turmeric powder

1 teaspoon coriander powder

1 teaspoon cumin powder

Salt to taste

1 sprig cilantro, finely chopped

METHOD

1. Heat the oil in a saucepan over medium heat for 1 minute. Add the asafetida and cumin seeds. When the cumin seeds begin to splutter, add the ginger, curry leaves, and cauliflower. Sauté, stirring occasionally, for about 5 minutes.

2. Reduce the heat. Add the turmeric, coriander, cumin, and salt and cook for about 10 minutes, until the cauliflower has softened.

3. Remove the pan from the heat. Sprinkle the mixture with cilantro and serve warm.

NOTE   Serve with whole-wheat tortilla or roti.

Paryank Asana
(Couch Pose)

Did You Know?   Three florets of cauliflower a day will provide 67 percent of the daily vitamin C requirement. Cauliflower is also known for containing folate, which helps the blood work more efficiently and is often recommended for preventing anemia.

paneer bhurji {Sattvic}

SERVES 2 ❧ *Preparation time: 20 minutes*

INGREDIENTS

1 teaspoon ghee or butter

One 1-inch piece of ginger, peeled
   and chopped

1 green bell pepper, diced

1 tomato, finely chopped

1 teaspoon roasted cumin powder

Pinch of turmeric powder

Salt to taste

2 cups low-fat cottage cheese or
   mashed paneer (Indian cheese)

1 teaspoon lemon juice

5 roasted cashews, chopped into
   small pieces

OPTIONAL—Rajasic variation:

1 green chili, finely chopped

1 onion, finely chopped

3 garlic cloves, finely chopped

Pinch of red chili powder

METHOD

1. Heat the ghee or butter in a saucepan over medium heat for
   1 minute. Add the ginger and bell pepper. For the Rajasic
   variation, also add the green chili, onion, and garlic. Sauté
   for about 5 minutes, until tender.

2. Add the tomato and cook for 2 minutes. Add the cumin,
   turmeric, and salt. For the Rajasic variation, also add the
   red chili powder.

3. Add the cottage cheese or paneer and mix well. Stir in the
   lemon juice.

4. Remove the pan from the heat. Garnish with cashews and
   serve.

NOTE Serve with whole-wheat tortilla or roti.

Did You Know? Cheese is a good source of high-quality protein,
calcium, and many other essential nutrients.

Pavan-Mukth Asana
(Wind-Releasing Pose)

gourd patties {Sattvic}

SERVES 2 ❖ *Preparation time: 20 minutes*

INGREDIENTS

1 small bottle gourd, peeled and
    finely grated
2 medium potatoes, about 5 ounces
    each, peeled, cooked, and mashed
Pinch of turmeric powder
1 teaspoon roasted cumin powder
Salt to taste
1 sprig cilantro, finely chopped
1 teaspoon lemon juice

METHOD

1. Preheat the oven to 450°F.
2. Combine the gourd and the mashed potatoes in a large mixing bowl. With your hands, knead the ingredients together until well combined.
3. Stir in the turmeric, cumin, and salt. Add the cilantro and lemon juice.
4. Shape the mixture into 4 patties. Place the patties on a greased baking sheet and bake for 20 minutes. Serve warm.

NOTE Serve with Cilantro-Mint Chutney (page 69).

Did You Know? Bottle gourd, also known as green squash or lauki, resembles a yellow crookneck squash in shape but is light green. It is excellent for balancing liver function and is often recommended when the liver is inflamed and cannot efficiently process food.

Paschi-Mottana Asana
(Seated Forward Bend)

corn curry {Sattvic}

SERVES 2 ❖ *Preparation time: 20 minutes*

INGREDIENTS

2 ears corn

1 tablespoon vegetable oil or ghee
   (Indian clarified butter)

Pinch of asafetida

1 teaspoon cumin seeds

Pinch of turmeric powder

1 teaspoon coriander powder

Salt to taste

½ cup nonfat or low-fat plain
   yogurt, whipped

1 sprig cilantro, chopped

OPTIONAL—Rajasic variation:

1 green chili, chopped

Pinch of red chili powder

METHOD

1. Using a sharp knife, remove the kernels from the corncobs and set them aside.

2. Heat the oil or ghee in a medium skillet over medium heat for 1 minute. Add the pinch of asafetida and the cumin seeds. For the Rajasic variation, also add the green chili. When the cumin seeds start to splutter, add the corn. Reduce the heat to medium-low and sauté the corn, stirring occasionally, for 5 minutes, or until partially tender.

3. Add the turmeric, coriander, and salt. For the Rajasic variation, also add the red chili powder. Mix well. Add 1 cup water and simmer, stirring occasionally, for 2 to 3 minutes.

4. Stir in the whipped yogurt and continue cooking for 5 minutes.

5. Remove the pan from the heat. Garnish the curry with cilantro and serve hot.

NOTE Serve with whole-wheat tortilla, roti, or basmati rice.

Ustra Asana
(Camel Pose)

Did You Know? Corn is a good source of vitamin C, fiber, folic acid, and thiamine (vitamin B1). It is known to be a heart protector.

broccoli and tofu {Sattvic}

SERVES 2 ❖ *Preparation time: 20 minutes*

INGREDIENTS

2 teaspoons sesame oil

¼ pound broccoli, cut into small florets

1 green bell pepper, cut into 1-inch squares

1 scallion, finely chopped

One 2-inch piece of ginger, peeled and chopped

¼ pound tofu, cut into 1-inch squares

1 teaspoon soy sauce

OPTIONAL—Rajasic variation:

2 garlic cloves, finely chopped

METHOD

1. Heat the sesame oil in a medium skillet over medium heat for 1 minute. Add the broccoli and bell pepper and cook for about 5 to 8 minutes, or until just tender.

2. Add the scallion and ginger. For the Rajasic variation, also add garlic. Cook for another minute.

3. Stir in the tofu and soy sauce. Cover the pan, reduce the heat to low, and cook for 10 minutes. Serve hot.

NOTE   Serve with whole-wheat tortilla or roti.

Did You Know?   Broccoli contains large amounts of vitamins C and K, calcium, and folate, and is known to contain antioxidants and several anticancer nutrients.

Vakra Asana III
(Twist Posture III)

masoor dal {Sattvic}

SERVES 2 ❖ *Preparation time: 35 minutes (pressure cooker); 60 minutes (stovetop)*

INGREDIENTS

1 cup red masoor lentils (available
    at Indian grocery stores)
1 tablespoon vegetable oil or ghee
    (Indian clarified butter)
Pinch of asafetida
1 teaspoon cumin seeds
1 tomato, chopped
One 1-inch piece of ginger, peeled
    and chopped
Pinch of turmeric powder
1 teaspoon coriander powder
Salt to taste
1 teaspoon lemon juice
1 sprig cilantro, finely chopped

METHOD

1. Combine the lentils and 4 cups water in a medium saucepan and bring to a boil over high heat. Reduce the heat and simmer for about 45 minutes, until the lentils are tender. Alternatively, to cook in half the time, you can use a pressure cooker using half the amount of water. Make sure to follow the manufacturer's instructions.

2. Heat the oil or ghee in a large saucepan over medium heat for 1 minute. Add the asafetida and cumin seeds. When the seeds start to splutter, add the tomato and ginger. Cook, stirring occasionally, for 5 minutes.

3. Add the cooked lentils, ½ cup water, the turmeric, coriander, and salt and cook, stirring occasionally, for 5 minutes.

4. Remove the pan from the heat and add the lemon juice.

5. Garnish with cilantro and serve.

NOTE Serve with basmati rice.

Hala Asana
(Plow Pose)

Did You Know? Cumin seeds are one of the main ingredients in curries. They can be used in the form of seeds or they can be roasted and powdered. A very popular seasoning, they are a good source of iron and an excellent digestive aid.

moong dal {Sattvic}

SERVES 2 ❖ *Preparation time: 40 minutes*

INGREDIENTS

1 cup yellow moong lentils

2 teaspoons vegetable oil or ghee
(Indian clarified butter)

Pinch of asafetida

1 teaspoon cumin seeds

One 1-inch piece of ginger, peeled
and finely chopped

Pinch of turmeric powder

1 teaspoon coriander powder

Salt to taste

1 sprig cilantro, finely chopped

OPTIONAL—Rajasic variation:

Pinch of red chili powder

METHOD

1. Combine the lentils and 3 cups water in a medium bowl. Soak for 10 minutes; drain. Set aside.

2. Heat the oil or ghee in a large saucepan over medium heat for 1 minute. Add the asafetida and cumin seeds. When the seeds begin to splutter, add the ginger and the lentils. Stir in the turmeric, coriander, and salt. For the Rajasic variation, also add the red chili powder.

3. Reduce the heat to medium-low and simmer, stirring occasionally, for 20 to 25 minutes, or until the lentils are soft.

4. Remove the pan from the heat. Sprinkle with cilantro and serve.

NOTES The same recipe can also be used to cook split green or black lentils.
❖ Serve with basmati rice.

Did You Know? Moong lentils, also known as the "king of lentils," have been used since Vedic times. A traditional yogic bean, known to sustain energy and strength, the moong lentil is considered to be one of the easiest lentils to digest and is a good source of protein. It is very low in fat and provides loads of fiber.

Ardh-Sarvang Asana
(Half Shoulder Stand)

white yogurt kadi {Sattvic}

SERVES 2 ❖ *Preparation time: 40 minutes*

INGREDIENTS

¾ cup nonfat plain yogurt

2 tablespoons chickpea flour

Salt to taste

2 teaspoons vegetable oil or ghee
 (Indian clarified butter)

Pinch of asafetida

I teaspoon mustard seeds

I teaspoon cumin seeds

½ teaspoon fenugreek seeds

2–3 whole cloves

One 2-inch piece of ginger, peeled
 and finely chopped

2–3 curry leaves

I sprig cilantro, finely chopped

METHOD

1. Combine the yogurt, chickpea flour, and 3 cups water in a medium bowl; whisk until blended. Season with salt.

2. Heat the oil or ghee in a saucepan over medium heat for I minute. Add the asafetida, mustard seeds, cumin, fenugreek, cloves, ginger, and curry leaves. Reduce the heat to low and gradually pour in the yogurt mixture. Cook, stirring, for 8 minutes, or until the liquid comes to a gentle boil.

3. Reduce the heat and simmer gently, stirring occasionally, for 25 to 30 minutes, or until the sauce begins to thicken to a custardlike consistency.

4. Remove the pan from the heat. Sprinkle the sauce with cilantro and serve.

NOTE Serve with white basmati rice.

Did You Know? Chickpea flour or gram flour, also known as "besan," is made by milling split bengal gram to a fine flour. It is used very widely in traditional Indian yogic food. It is not only protein-rich, but also known to improve health by lowering blood cholesterol, helping with diseases such as diabetes, and stimulating sexual potency. Combined with yogurt, it is easy to digest.

Sarvang Asana
(Shoulder Stand)

rice

GREEN PULAV

YELLOW LEMON RICE

YOGURT RICE

MINT PULAV

VEGETABLE PULAV

MOONG KICHDI

GREEN LENTIL AND RICE KICHDI

green pulav {Sattvic}

SERVES 2 ❧ *Preparation time: 30 minutes*

INGREDIENTS

1 large bunch cilantro, chopped

1 green bell pepper, chopped

One 1-inch piece of ginger, peeled
and chopped

1 tablespoon vegetable oil or ghee
(Indian clarified butter)

2 sticks cinnamon

2 whole cloves

3 cardamom pods, split open

2 bay leaves

1 cup uncooked basmati rice, soaked
in 2 cups water (soaking liquid
reserved)

¼ pound cauliflower, chopped

¼ pound broccoli, chopped

½ potato, peeled and diced

¼ cup fresh, shelled green peas

Salt to taste

OPTIONAL—Rajasic variation:

3 cloves garlic, peeled

1 green chili

METHOD

1. Combine the cilantro, bell pepper, and ginger in a blender. For the Rajasic version, also add the garlic and green chili. Grind the mixture into a paste.

2. Heat the oil or ghee in a sauté pan over medium heat for 1 minute. Add the cinnamon, cloves, cardamom pods, and bay leaves. Stir in the cilantro paste and cook, stirring occasionally, for 5 minutes.

3. Add the rice, reserved soaking liquid, cauliflower, broccoli, potato, peas, and salt; mix well. Reduce the heat to low and simmer, covered, for 10 to 12 minutes, until the rice has absorbed all the liquid and the vegetables are tender.

4. Remove the pan from the heat and serve hot.

NOTE Serve with low-fat plain yogurt or White Yogurt Kadi (page 95).

Did You Know? Ghee (Indian clarified butter) is the purest form of butterfat. It is mentioned in ancient holy Indian texts as the best form of oil for cooking. Although it has a high fat content, when used in moderation, it stimulates the digestion better than any other oil and is recommended in yoga. It is also known to strengthen the immune system. Ghee can be stored for long periods of time and does not require refrigeration.

Vrks Asana
(Tree Pose)

yellow lemon rice {Sattvic}

SERVES 2 ❧ *Preparation time: 15 minutes*

INGREDIENTS

1 tablespoon vegetable oil

Pinch of asafetida

1 teaspoon mustard seeds

2 cups cooked basmati rice

Pinch of turmeric powder

Salt to taste

1 tablespoon lemon juice

Leaves from 1 sprig cilantro, finely
     chopped

OPTIONAL—*Rajasic variation:*

Pinch of red chili powder

METHOD

1. Heat the oil in a skillet over medium heat for 1 minute. Add the asafetida and mustard seeds. When the seeds start to splutter, add the rice and reduce the heat to low.

2. Stir in the turmeric and salt. For the Rajasic variation, also add the red chili powder. Mix well. Cook, stirring occasionally, for 5 minutes.

3. Remove the pan from the heat and add the lemon juice. Sprinkle with cilantro and serve.

NOTE   Serve with Vegetable Raita (page 64).

Did You Know?   Turmeric powder is used in a myriad of Indian dishes. In addition to imparting great aroma and flavor, turmeric has many medicinal properties. Its rich iron content serves as a blood purifier and is also known to improve liver function, prevent coughs and colds, and improve skin tone. It possesses anti-inflammatory properties and is a powerful antioxidant and antiseptic.

Simha Asana
(Lion Pose)

yogurt rice {Sattvic}

SERVES 2 ❖ *Preparation time: 15 minutes*

INGREDIENTS

1 tablespoon vegetable oil

Pinch of asafetida

1 teaspoon mustard seeds

3–4 small curry leaves

2 cups cooked basmati rice

1 cup nonfat or low-fat plain yogurt

Salt to taste

1 sprig cilantro, finely chopped

METHOD

1. Heat the oil in a skillet over medium heat for 1 minute. Add the asafetida and mustard seeds. When the seeds start to splutter, add the curry leaves. Stir in the rice and yogurt. Season with salt; mix well. Cook, stirring occasionally, for 5 minutes.

2. Garnish with cilantro and serve.

NOTE   Serve with Bean Sprout Salad (page 54).

Vajra Asana
(Thunderbolt Pose)

Did You Know?   Mustard—usually used in seed, paste, or powdered form—has been popular since Vedic and medieval times. Mustard seeds have digestive, laxative, antiseptic, and circulative stimulant properties. As a digestive aid, mustard, in moderation, neutralizes toxins and helps ward off an upset stomach.

mint pulav {Sattvic}

SERVES 2 ❖ *Preparation time: 45 minutes*

INGREDIENTS

1 cup uncooked basmati rice, rinsed
    and drained several times

1 tablespoon vegetable oil or ghee
    (Indian clarified butter)

One 1-inch piece of cinnamon stick

2 bay leaves

3 whole cloves

2 cardamom pods, split open

One 1-inch piece of ginger, peeled
    and crushed

½ cup low-fat or nonfat plain
    yogurt, well stirred

Salt to taste

1 cup (about 1 bunch) mint leaves,
    finely chopped

METHOD

1. In a small bowl, combine the rice and 2 cups water; soak for 20 minutes.

2. Heat the oil or ghee in a sauté pan over medium heat for 1 minute. Add the cinnamon stick, bay leaves, cloves, cardamom pods, and ginger. Stir in the yogurt and cook for 2 minutes.

3. Transfer the rice, along with its soaking liquid, to the pan. Add salt and bring to a boil. When the mixture begins to simmer, stir in the mint leaves. Reduce the heat, cover, and continue to simmer for 10 to 12 minutes, or until the rice is tender.

4. Serve hot.

NOTE Serve with low-fat plain yogurt.

Did You Know? Mint adds a distinctive fresh flavor and aroma to food and is often used to ease stomach disorders, kidney problems, and bronchitis.

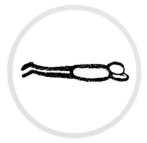

Makra Asana
(Crocodile Pose)

vegetable pulav {Sattvic}

SERVES 2 ❖ *Preparation time: 30 minutes*

INGREDIENTS

1 tablespoon vegetable oil or ghee
   (Indian clarified butter)

2 cardamom pods, split open

One 1-inch piece of cinnamon stick

2 whole cloves

3–4 cashews, finely chopped

1 bay leaf

8 French beans, thinly sliced
   lengthwise

¼ cup fresh, shelled green peas

¼ cup small cauliflower florets

1 carrot, peeled and thinly sliced

1 cup uncooked basmati rice, rinsed
   and drained several times

Salt to taste

METHOD

1. Heat the oil or ghee in a sauté pan over medium heat for 1 minute. Add the cardamom pods, cinnamon, cloves, cashews, and bay leaf. Add the beans, peas, cauliflower, and carrot and sauté for 2 minutes.

2. Stir in the rice, 2 cups water, and salt. Reduce the heat to low and cover. Cook for about 15 minutes, until the water has been absorbed and the rice is tender.

3. Serve hot.

NOTE   Serve with Vegetable Raita (page 64).

Did You Know?   Cardamom is one of the ancient medicines of the world. It is used as a digestive aid, antispasmodic, aphrodisiac, and expectorant. It is also known to possess mild analgesic and anti-inflammatory properties. Cardamom is taken for coughs and respiratory allergies. It also helps control various digestive problems and urinary tract infections.

Dradh Asana
(Firm Side Pose)

moong kichdi {Sattvic}

SERVES 2 ❧ *Preparation time: 40 minutes (pressure cooker); 55 minutes (stovetop)*

INGREDIENTS

½ cup split yellow moong lentils
½ cup uncooked basmati rice
Pinch of turmeric powder
Salt to taste
1 tablespoon vegetable oil or ghee
   (Indian clarified butter)
1 teaspoon mustard seeds
1 teaspoon peeled and finely
   chopped ginger
2 teaspoons lemon juice
2 cilantro sprigs, finely chopped

METHOD

1. Combine the lentils and rice in a small bowl; with cold water rinse and drain three times. In a large pot, combine the mixture with 4 cups water and allow it to soak for 15 minutes.

2. Add the turmeric and salt, then bring the water to a boil over medium heat. Reduce the heat to low and simmer for 30 minutes, until the mixture is soft and sticky. Alternatively, you can use a pressure cooker, following the manufacturer's instructions (this will take half as much water).

3. Heat the oil or ghee in a large skillet over medium heat for 1 minute. Add the mustard seeds. When the seeds start to splutter, add the ginger.

4. Pour the rice and lentil mixture into the skillet, mix well, and cook, stirring occasionally, for 5 minutes.

5. Remove the skillet from the heat and add the lemon juice. Transfer the mixture to a serving dish and garnish with cilantro. Serve hot.

NOTE   Serve with White Yogurt Kadi (page 95).

Nishpand-Bhav Asana
(Relaxation Pose)

Did You Know?   Rice remains a staple food for more than two-thirds of the world's population. Rice is naturally fat-, cholesterol-, and sodium-free.

green lentil and rice kichdi {Sattvic}

SERVES 2 ❖ *Preparation time: 50 minutes (pressure cooker); 60 minutes (stovetop)*

INGREDIENTS

¾ cup split green lentils

¾ cup uncooked basmati rice

½ teaspoon turmeric powder

Salt to taste

1 tablespoon vegetable oil or ghee
    (Indian clarified butter)

Pinch of asafetida

1 teaspoon cumin seeds

One 1-inch piece of ginger, peeled
    and finely chopped

1 teaspoon roasted cumin powder

2 teaspoons lemon juice

2 sprigs cilantro, finely chopped

OPTIONAL—Rajasic variation:

2 garlic cloves, finely chopped

2 small green chilies, finely chopped

Shav Asana
(Corpse Pose)

METHOD

1. Combine the lentils and rice in a small bowl; with cold water, rinse and drain three times. In a medium saucepan, combine the mixture with 5 cups water and allow it to soak for 15 minutes.

2. Add the turmeric and salt and bring to a boil over medium heat. Reduce the heat and simmer for 20 to 25 minutes, until the lentils and rice are very tender and sticky. Alternatively, you can use a pressure cooker, following the manufacturer's instructions (this will take half as much water).

3. Remove the pan from the heat and allow the mixture to cool for 10 minutes.

4. Heat the oil or ghee in a skillet over medium heat for 1 minute. Add the asafetida and cumin seeds. When the seeds start to splutter, add the ginger and roasted cumin powder. For the Rajasic variation, also add the garlic and green chilies. Pour the rice and lentil mixture into the skillet, and stir well. Cook, stirring occasionally, for 5 minutes.

5. Cool, then add the lemon juice. Garnish with cilantro and serve.

NOTE Serve with White Yogurt Kadi (page 95) or Vegetable Raita (page 64).

Did You Know? Kichdi, a nourishing and delicious dish of rice and lentils cooked with ghee and spices, is one of the staples of the yogic diet. It is served in every ashram for good health, easy digestion, or rejuvenation therapy. Not only is it healthy, but it also enables the body to rest, recuperate, and cleanse itself of any toxins.

desserts

MANGO SRIKHAND

RICE PUDDING

APPLE MOUSSE

CARROT HALWA

SEMOLINA SHEERA

SAGO PUDDING

ORANGE CHEESE SANDESH

HONEY FRUIT DELIGHT

COCONUT BURFI

mango srikhand {Sattvic}

SERVES 2 ✤ *Preparation time: 15 minutes, plus draining and chilling time*

INGREDIENTS

2 cups nonfat plain yogurt

1 cup fresh mango pulp (the pureed
flesh of about 2 mangoes)

1 tablespoon organic sugar

½ teaspoon cardamom powder

4–5 threads saffron, soaked in
1 tablespoon warm water

1 teaspoon chopped pistachios

METHOD

1. Pour the yogurt into a muslin- or cheesecloth-lined sieve
set over a bowl. Let drain for 3 to 4 hours, to remove excess
liquid.

2. Pour the mango pulp into a second sieve to remove most of
its liquid.

3. Combine the mango and the yogurt in a dry bowl. Whip the
mixture until smooth and creamy. Add the sugar, cardamom,
and saffron; mix well.

4. Transfer the mixture to a serving bowl, cover, and chill for
3 to 4 hours.

5. Serve in individual dessert bowls, topped with a sprinkling
of pistachios.

Did You Know? Mango is considered to be the king of fruits. An average-size mango contains up to 40 percent of the daily fiber requirement. Dietary fiber is known to help protect against degenerative diseases, especially those affecting the heart, and it may help prevent certain types of cancer and lower blood cholesterol levels. Mango is an excellent source of vitamins A and C. It is rich in minerals and antioxidants and contains enzymes with stomach-soothing properties.

Pranayam I
(Breathing I)

rice pudding {Rajasic}

SERVES 4 ❖ *Preparation time: 40 minutes*

INGREDIENTS

10 cups low-fat milk

½ cup uncooked basmati rice,
    rinsed well and drained

⅓ cup organic sugar

½ teaspoon cardamom powder

4–5 threads saffron, soaked in
    1 tablespoon warm water

8–10 almonds, finely chopped

8–10 pistachios, finely copped

1 tablespoon small raisins

METHOD

1. Bring the milk to a simmer in a large pot over medium-low heat. Add the rice. Reduce the heat to low and cook, stirring every 5 minutes, for 30 minutes, until the rice is tender. Make sure the rice is quite soft before you continue.

2. Add the sugar and continue to cook for 5 minutes.

3. Stir in the cardamom, saffron, almonds, pistachios, and raisins. Remove the pudding from the heat.

4. Serve the pudding warm or chilled.

Pranayam II
(Breathing II)

Did You Know? Nuts such as almonds are rich in vitamin E, magnesium, zinc, selenium, copper, potassium, phosphorus, biotin, riboflavin, niacin, and iron and are an excellent source of fiber. ❖ Raisins are cholesterol-free, low in sodium, and fat-free. They provide many necessary vitamins and minerals, including iron, potassium, calcium, and certain B vitamins, including B1, B2, B3, B6, and B12. Raisins are a good source of fiber and are rich in antioxidants. They are 70 percent pure fructose (a natural form of sugar), which is easily digested for quick energy.

apple mousse {Rajasic}

SERVES 4 ❖ *Preparation time: 30 minutes, plus chilling time*

INGREDIENTS

1 tablespoon butter

3 pounds apples (unpeeled), cored and chopped

¼ cup organic sugar

Grated zest of 1 lemon

METHOD

1. Melt the butter in a saucepan over medium heat. Add the apples, and cook, stirring frequently, for 5 to 8 minutes, until soft.

2. While stirring, mash the apples and sprinkle them with the sugar. Continue cooking for about 5 minutes, until the apple mixture is soft and thick. Remove the pan from the heat and allow the apple to cool.

3. Press the cooked apple mixture through a sieve into a bowl and discard the peels.

4. Stir in the lemon zest and mix well.

5. Pour the mousse into a serving dish, cover, and chill for at least 30 minutes before serving.

Did You Know? Apples contain high amounts of vitamin C and folic acid, and they are an excellent source of dietary fiber and potassium. They also contain flavonoids, some of the most potent antioxidants.

Pranayam III
(Breathing III)

carrot halwa {Rajasic}

SERVES 4 ❖ *Preparation time: 45 minutes*

INGREDIENTS

5 cups low-fat milk

2 pounds carrots, peeled and grated

⅓ cup organic sugar

15–20 small raisins

8–10 roasted almonds, finely
   chopped

METHOD

1. In a large saucepan, bring the milk to a simmer over medium-low heat. Reduce the heat to low and add the grated carrots. Cook, stirring frequently, for 30 minutes, or until the milk has been completely absorbed.

2. Add the sugar and continue cooking, stirring more frequently to prevent sticking, for about 10 minutes, until the mixture becomes very thick.

3. Remove the pan from the heat and stir in the raisins.

4. Transfer the halwa to a serving bowl and sprinkle with almonds. Serve warm or chilled.

Did You Know? Carrots have powerful antioxidants that can boost the immune system and prevent cell degeneration. They are believed to provide special nutrition for the eyes and skin.

Pranayam IV
(Breathing IV)

semolina sheera {Rajasic}

SERVES 4 ❖ *Preparation time: 20 minutes*

INGREDIENTS

2 tablespoons ghee
   (Indian clarified butter)
1 cup semolina
½ cup organic sugar
8–10 almonds, finely chopped

METHOD

1. Heat the ghee in a small skillet over medium heat for 1 minute. Add the semolina and cook, stirring continuously, for 3 to 4 minutes, until it turns golden brown.
2. Gradually add 2½ cups boiling water, stirring, and continue to cook for about 3 minutes, until the mixture has thickened.
3. Add the sugar. Reduce the heat to low and cook, stirring often to prevent sticking, for 5 minutes.
4. Transfer the sheera to a serving bowl and garnish with almonds. Serve hot.

Pranayam V
(Breathing V)

Did You Know? Semolina and other wheat products help to boost energy and enhance physical strength and endurance.

sago pudding {Rajasic}

SERVES 4 ❖ *Preparation time: 40 minutes*

INGREDIENTS

4 cups milk

½ cup sago, rinsed well and drained

½ cup organic sugar

METHOD

1. Bring the milk to a simmer in a large saucepan over medium heat. Add the sago and stir well. Reduce the heat and cook, stirring frequently, for 30 minutes, or until the sago is tender and spongy and the milk has thickened.
2. Add the sugar and continue to cook, stirring, for 3 minutes.
3. Remove the pan from the heat and serve the pudding warm.

Did You Know?   Sago, also known as white tapioca or sabudana, looks somewhat like the familiar tapioca, although the two foods are not related. The small pearllike balls soften when cooked in water or milk. Sago is completely fat- and cholesterol-free.

Relaxing Eyes

orange cheese sandesh {Rajasic}

SERVES 4 ❖ *Preparation time: 15 minutes, plus chilling time*

INGREDIENTS

2 cups low-fat cottage cheese

½ cup organic sugar

2 tablespoons orange juice

1 orange

METHOD

1. Peel the orange and remove every scrap of the bitter white pith. Cut between the segments to separate them. Set aside.

2. Combine the cottage cheese and sugar in a medium bowl. With a spoon or whisk, beat until well blended. Transfer the mixture to a saucepan and cook, stirring continuously, over low heat, for 5 minutes.

3. Remove the pan from the heat and allow the mixture to cool.

4. Stir in the orange juice. Spread the cheese mixture in an even layer on a plate. Arrange the orange segments on top of the cheese mixture. Cover and chill the dessert for 30 minutes.

5. Cut into squares and serve.

Relaxing Ears

Did You Know?   Milk and milk products contain calcium, potassium, and magnesium, all of which may lower the risk of serious illnesses. It is healthier to consume low-fat or nonfat milk products; there is no difference in their nutritive value except for their lower fat content, which means they have fewer calories than whole-milk products.

honey fruit delight {Sattvic}

SERVES 4 ❖ *Preparation time: 15 minutes, plus chilling time*

INGREDIENTS

2 oranges

1 grapefruit

2 tablespoons honey

3 tablespoons lemon juice

2 kiwifruits

1 banana

½ cup strawberries, hulled and
    thinly sliced

2 tablespoons chopped pistachios

METHOD

1. Peel the oranges and grapefruit and remove every scrap of the bitter white pith. Cut between the segments to separate them and place the segments in a serving bowl.
2. In a small bowl, whisk together the honey and lemon juice. Pour the mixture over the orange and grapefruit segments.
3. Peel the kiwifruits and cut them into thick slices. Add them to the bowl and toss well. Cover and chill the mixture for 1 hour.
4. When you are ready to serve, peel and slice the banana and toss it with the other fruits.
5. Garnish with the strawberries and pistachios and serve.

Did You Know? Honey is of great value for digestive disturbances. It is known to be an excellent reconstructive tonic for anemics, dyspeptics, convalescents, and the aged.

Relaxing Neck and Shoulders

coconut burfi {Rajasic}

SERVES 4 ❖ *Preparation time: 40 minutes, plus cooling time*

INGREDIENTS

4 cups low-fat milk

2 cups grated fresh coconut

¾ cup organic sugar

6 threads saffron, soaked in
    I tablespoon warm water

I teaspoon ghee
    (Indian clarified butter)

METHOD

I. Bring the milk to simmer in a large saucepan over medium-low heat. Add the coconut and stir well. Cook, stirring continuously, about 30 minutes, until the coconut is almost dry.

2. Add the sugar and saffron and continue cooking, stirring, for 5 to 7 minutes, or until the mixture becomes quite sticky. Remove the pan from the heat.

3. Grease an 8-by-8-inch baking pan with the ghee and spread the coconut mixture evenly in the pan. Let sit at room temperature for 30 minutes.

4. Cut the burfi into square- or diamond-shaped pieces and serve.

Relaxing Tongue

Did You Know? Coconut is a good source of iron and vitamin E. It is cooling to the body, boosts energy, and is known to enhance sexual potency.

Asana Index

Yoga postures (asanas) help to build a strong, healthy, flexible, and well-toned body. They raise physical awareness of the body, muscles, and breath. Proper breathing techniques are essential to the practice of yoga, and the combination of breath inhalation and exhalation allows tense muscles to relax and send soothing messages to the brain that help balance the mind and body. These postures help to keep the body supple, stretch the spine, strengthen the muscles, massage the vital organs, and improve relaxation.

Points to Remember:

✤ *Your daily yoga exercise should not exceed one hour.*

✤ *Do not eat during the hour before you practice yoga postures.*

✤ *Many yoga poses require regular practice, patience, determination, and fortitude to achieve. Do not expect to be able to do them immediately. For each pose, challenge yourself to do as much as you can at that moment without strain. Over time you will acquire the strength and flexibility needed to accomplish the full pose.*

The following sixty-two yoga postures can be practiced in addition to cooking and consuming yogic food.

1. OM CHANT I

✤ Sit or stand in a comfortable position, arms relaxed at your sides. Relax your mind and breathe normally.

✤ Chant the word "om" as follows: While inhaling, stress the "o" sound for as long as possible. Exhale at the "m" sound. (It should sound like "ooooooooomm.")

✤ Repeat 3 times.

Benefits: Prepares you for yoga.

2. OM CHANT II

✤ Sit or stand in a comfortable position, arms relaxed at your sides. Relax your mind and breathe normally.

✤ Chant the word "om" as follows: While inhaling, chant "om." Place the stress on the "m" sound. Hold the breath while making this sound for as long as possible. (It should sound like "oommmmmmmm.")

✤ Repeat three times.

Benefits: Prepares you for yoga.

3. SUKH ASANA
(Easy Pose)

✤ Sit cross-legged on a mat with your spine erect, abdomen drawn in, and head poised.

✤ Place your hands, palms downward, on your knees. Close your eyes and rid your body of all tension.

✤ Breathe normally. Concentrate on the breath, shutting out all thoughts.

Benefits: Corrects posture; increases flexibility of knees and ankles; establishes inner harmony, reducing muscle tension; prepares you for yoga.

4. STHITH-PRARTHANA ASANA
(Standing Prayer Pose)

✤ Stand erect with your feet together, elbows and shoulders relaxed.

✤ Press your palms together and place them at the base of the sternum.

✤ Close your eyes and remain steady. Breathe normally.

Benefits: Helps correct posture; improves balance and poise; prepares you for yoga.

5. YONI MUDRA
(Yogic Seal)

✤ Sit in Sukh Asana (pose 3) or Padma Asana (pose 13).

✤ Place your hands on your face, thumbs covering your ears and index fingers closing your eyelids. Use the middle fingers to close your nostrils, place the ring fingers on your upper lip, and place the little fingers on your lower lip.

✤ Relax and breathe normally.

Benefits: Helps to achieve internal equilibrium and concentration and to control senses.

6. ARDH-PADMA ASANA
(Half-Lotus Pose)

✤ Sit on a mat, stretching your legs forward. Fold one leg and place your foot on the opposite thigh. Fold your other leg and place that foot as close to the opposite thigh as possible. Your knees should be touching the ground—apply a little pressure, if necessary.

✤ Place your hands on your knees. Your chest, neck, and spine should be erect, and your abdomen should be slightly pulled in.

✤ Close your eyes and relax.

Benefits: Increases lower-body flexibility; aids meditation; promotes physical and mental relaxation.

7. YOGA MUDRA
(Symbol of Yoga)

✤ Assume Sukh Asana (pose 3), sit erect, and bring one arm behind your back to hold the wrist of your other hand.

✤ Exhale for 3 seconds while gently bending down to touch your right knee with your forehead or nose. Hold your breath for 6 seconds. Inhale for 3 seconds while returning to upright position.

✤ Repeat these steps for the left knee.

✤ Perform three sets alternately on each side. Finish by doing one more set, this time touching your forehead to the center, on the ground.

Benefits: Loosens posterior muscles of spinal column; improves upper-body circulation; massages internal organs; eases flatulence and constipation.

8. GARUD ASANA
(Eagle Pose)

✤ Stand erect with your feet together and arms relaxed at your sides. Cross your right arm behind the left, interlocking your elbows and placing your palms together. Wrap your right leg around your left leg, interlocking your knees and ankles.

✤ Hold the position and breathe normally.

✤ Repeat the steps for the other side.

Benefits: Strengthens muscles; develops concentration, poise, self-confidence, and physical stability.

9. TAL ASANA I
(Tree Pose I)

✤ Stand erect with your feet about 1 foot apart, hands at your sides. Keep your spine and neck straight and your abdomen in normal contour.

✤ Inhale for 3 seconds while raising one arm and your heels simultaneously to rise onto your toes. Maintain this pose, holding your breath for 6 seconds.

✤ Exhale and bring the raised arm down, rotating it backward to the starting position while simultaneously lowering your heels.

✤ Repeat for the other arm. Do three sets.

Benefits: Stretches the body and improves blood circulation; expands lung capacity.

10. TAL ASANA II
(Tree Pose II)

✤ Stand erect with your feet about 1 foot apart, hands at your sides. Keep your spine and neck straight and your abdomen in normal contour.

✤ Inhale for 3 seconds while raising both arms and heels simultaneously to rise onto your toes. Maintain this pose, holding your breath for 6 seconds.

✤ Exhale and bring your arms down, rotating them backward to the starting position while simultaneously lowering your heels.

✤ Do three sets.

Benefits: Stretches the body and improves blood circulation; expands lung capacity; indirectly massages the abdominal organs.

11. GOMUKH ASANA
(Cow Face Pose)

✤ Sit on a mat with your legs outstretched. Bend your left leg so that your heel touches your right hip. Bend your right leg so that your right knee is above your left knee and your right heel touches your left hip. Your feet should face outward to either side.

✤ Raise your right arm and bend it backward with the elbow pointing up to touch the middle of your back. Bend your left arm behind your waist and upward to clasp your right hand. Interlock your fingers.

✤ Breathe normally, keeping your spine, back, and neck erect and in line, for 6 seconds.

✤ Reverse the position so that your left knee is on top and your left arm is bent above. Do three sets, alternating left and right sides.

Benefits: Brings flexibility to the extremities; improves shoulder position.

12. PARVAT ASANA I
(Seated Mountain Pose I)

✤ Sit in Sukh Asana (pose 3) or Padma Asana (pose 13) with your hands straight at your sides.

✤ Inhale for 3 seconds, raising both hands simultaneously and joining your palms above your head. Make sure your elbows are straight and your arms are close to your ears.

✤ Keep your back erect and tighten your abdomen slightly. Maintain the position while holding your breath for 6 seconds. Exhale for 3 seconds while bringing your arms down.

✤ Repeat twice more.

Benefits: Flexes hip joints; straightens back muscles.

13. PADMA ASANA
(Lotus Pose)

✤ Sit on the mat with your legs stretched forward. Fold one leg and place the foot on the opposite thigh. Fold the other leg and place that foot on the other thigh. Your knees should be touching the ground—apply a little pressure, if necessary.

✤ Place your hands on your knees. Your chest, neck, and spine should be erect, and your abdomen should be slightly pulled in.

✤ Relax your face muscles; maintain calm. Place your right hand, palm facing up, near your navel. Place your left hand, palm facing up, on the back of your right hand.

✤ Close your eyes and concentrate on a point between your eyebrows.

Benefits: Increases lower-body flexibility; aids meditation; promotes physical and mental relaxation.

14. EKPAD ASANA
(One-Leg Pose)

✤ Stand erect with your feet together and arms at your sides, eyes focused forward.

✤ Place your right foot on the inner thigh of your left leg. Join hands with palms together near your breastbone.

✤ Breathe normally, holding the pose for 1 minute. Repeat with the other leg.

Benefits: Relaxes the leg muscles; aids nerve control; teaches balance; helps concentration.

15. UTKAT ASANA
(Powerful Pose)

✤ Stand erect with your feet about 1 foot apart, arms at your sides. Inhale for 3 seconds, rising on your toes and bringing both hands forward in line with your shoulders, palms facing down. Hold your breath for 3 seconds.

✤ Exhale for 3 seconds, remaining on your toes while bending at the knees to sit on your heels. Hold the pose for 6 seconds.

✤ Inhale for 3 seconds, rising to stand on your toes, and hold your breath for 3 seconds.

✤ Exhale for 3 seconds, lowering your heels and returning to the starting position.

Benefits: Strengthens legs and abdominal and pelvic muscles; improves muscular coordination and balance; stimulates blood circulation.

16. TRIKON ASANA VARIATION
(Triangle Pose Variation)

✤ Stand erect with your feet together. Inhale for 2 seconds while raising both arms in front of you to shoulder level.

✤ Exhale for 2 seconds, bending from the waist to touch your toes while keeping your back erect. Keep your head up and your eyes fixed on your nose. Maintain the pose and hold your breath for 4 seconds.

✤ Inhale for 2 seconds, returning to the starting position.

Benefits: Corrects faulty posture; exercises spine and back muscles; increases flexibility of waist and tones abdominal muscles.

17. TAL ASANA III
(Tree Pose III)

✤ Stand erect, hands at your sides, spine and neck straight, and abdomen in normal contour.

✤ Inhale for 3 seconds, crossing your arms in front of you and raising them overhead while simultaneously rising on your toes. Maintain this position, holding your breath, for 6 seconds.

✤ Exhale and return to the starting position, simultaneously lowering your heels. Do three sets.

Benefits: Stretches the entire body and expands lung capacity; develops respiratory muscles and massages internal organs; teaches a balanced state of mind.

18. KON ASANA I
(Angle Pose I)

✤ Stand erect with your feet about 2 feet apart and parallel. Place your right hand above your waist and your left hand on the side of your left thigh. Turn your head to look down along your left leg.

✤ Inhale for 3 seconds while sliding your left hand as far as possible toward your ankle and bringing your right hand farther upward. (Make sure not to bend your body forward or backward, and do not bend your knees. Focus your eyes on the hand on the thigh.) Remain in this position, holding your breath, for 6 seconds.

✤ Exhale for 3 seconds while returning to the starting position.

✤ Repeat for the opposite side. Do three sets, alternating sides.

Benefits: Stretches the spine laterally and gives greater elasticity to the vertebral column;

reduces fat and maintains the flexibility of the waist; massages abdominal organs such as the liver, stomach, and pancreas.

19. KON ASANA II
(Angle Pose II)

✤ Stand erect with your feet about 2 feet apart and parallel. Raise your right arm above your head, touching your ear. Place your left hand on your left thigh.

✤ Inhale for 3 seconds while bending sideways to the left. Stretch your right arm as if trying to make it parallel to the ground, and slide your left hand down toward your ankle. Remain in this position, holding your breath, for 6 seconds.

✤ Exhale for 3 seconds and return to the starting position. Repeat for the other side. Do three sets, alternating sides.

Benefits: All benefits of Kon Asana I; reduces muscular pain.

20. KON ASANA III
(Angle Pose III)

✤ Stand erect with your feet about 2 feet apart and parallel. Stretch your arms wide apart at shoulder level with your palms facing upward.

✤ Inhale for 3 seconds and lean slightly backward. Exhale on a count of 3 seconds and bend down to touch your left toe with your right hand. Keep your left hand extended straight above your head, in line with your ear. Turn your face upward to look at your left arm. Remain in this position, holding your breath, for 6 seconds.

✤ Inhale for 3 seconds while returning to the starting position. Repeat for the other side. Do three sets, alternating sides.

Benefits: Strengthens the spine; exercises the neck and extremities; corrects weak back muscles and drooping shoulders; massages internal organs; helps to achieve humility through exertion.

21. CHAKRA ASANA VARIATION
(Wheel Pose Variation)

✤ Stand erect with your feet about 18 inches apart and your arms at your sides.

✤ Inhale for 3 seconds, raising your arms to interlock your fingers. Arch your back and pause, holding your breath, for 6 seconds.

❖ Exhale for 3 seconds, bending forward and swinging your arms behind and above your shoulders to interlock your fingers at your back. Inhale for 3 seconds, returning to the starting position.

Benefits: Stretches the spine, massages internal organs, and helps muscular back pain; builds flexibility and confidence.

22. ARDHA MATSYA ASANA
(Fish Pose)

❖ Lie on your back with your legs straight and arms at your sides. Place your left foot on your right thigh near the pelvic region and gently press your left knee toward the ground.

❖ Maintain this position for as long as possible. Breathe normally.

❖ Repeat for the opposite side.

❖ Optional—Once this pose is comfortable, try doing the pose with both legs bent for a maximum of 2 minutes.

Benefits: Releases pain in the hip area and lower extremities; increases flexibility.

23. HASTPAD ASANA
(Hands to Feet Pose)

❖ Stand erect with your feet together.

❖ Inhale for 3 seconds and stretch your arms above your head. Tilt your torso slightly backward while keeping your knees straight.

❖ Exhale for 3 seconds and bend forward, keeping your knees straight, to hold your ankles. Your head should face down below your knees. Remain in this position, without breathing, for 6 seconds. Inhale for 3 seconds while returning to the starting position.

Benefits: Keeps the spine supple; provides maximum stretch to posterior muscles; massages intra-abdominal organs; encourages the experience of egolessness.

24. VAKRA ASANA II
(Twist Posture II)

❖ Sit on the floor with your legs stretching forward, knees together, and back straight. Inhale, stretching the arms at shoulder level, parallel to the floor, palms facing down.

❖ Exhale, twisting your body from the waist as far as possible, moving your arms and head together to the right.

✤ Inhale to return to the starting position, then repeat for the opposite side. Do two sets.
Benefits: Flexes the vertebral column and shoulder joints; increases the flexibility of the waist.

25. PARVAT ASANA II
(Seated Mountain Pose II)

✤ Sit in Sukh Asana (pose 3) or Padma Asana (pose 13) with your hands straight at your sides.

✤ Inhale for 3 seconds, raising both hands simultaneously and placing the palms together above your head. Keep your elbows straight and your arms close to the ears. Hold your back erect and tighten your abdomen slightly.

✤ Tilt to the right side as far as possible and maintain the position while holding your breath for 6 seconds.

✤ Exhale for 3 seconds, returning to the starting position. Repeat on the left side.
Benefits: Flexes the hip joints; straightens the back muscles; helps reduce fat around the abdomen.

26. BHADRA ASANA
(Throne Pose)

✤ Sit on the floor with your legs stretching forward and back straight.

✤ Inhale for 3 seconds while keeping your legs in contact with the floor, then draw your feet toward the groin, place the soles of your feet together, and gently push your knees down.

✤ Lock your hands over your feet and pull inward, keeping your body erect. Remain in this pose, holding your breath, for 6 seconds.

✤ Exhale for 3 seconds and return to the starting position. Repeat twice more.
Benefits: Stretches the inner thighs and strengthens the pelvic muscles; helps achieve stability.

27. PARVAT ASANA III
(Seated Mountain Pose III)

✤ Sit in Sukh Asana (pose 3) or Padma Asana (pose 13) with your hands straight at your sides.

✤ Inhale for 3 seconds, raising both hands simultaneously and placing your palms together above your head. Keep your elbows straight and your arms close to your ears.

Hold your back erect and tighten your abdomen slightly.

✤ Exhale for 3 seconds, bending forward with your arms pulling as strongly to the front as possible—keep your arms 6 inches from the ground. Maintain the position while holding your breath for 6 seconds. Inhale for 3 seconds, returning to the starting position.

Benefits: Flexes the hip joints; straightens the back muscles; helps reduce fat around the abdomen; promotes stability, elevation, and self-expression.

28. SHALABH ASANA
(Locust Pose)

✤ Lie on your stomach with your arms alongside your body and palms facing down.

✤ Exhale for 2 seconds, lifting your right leg straight up as far as possible without bending your knee. Remain in this position, holding your breath, for 4 seconds.

✤ Repeat with the left leg. Then repeat with both legs at once.

Benefits: Strengthens the lower back; reduces fat on the thighs; increases confidence.

29. YASTIK ASANA
(Stick Pose)

✤ Lie on your back with your legs fully extended, toes pointed, and arms at your sides.

✤ Inhale for 3 seconds, raising your arms until they are fully outstretched over the head. Stretch your whole body, making sure your arms and toes stretch as far as possible.

✤ Maintain the position while holding your breath for 6 seconds. Exhale for 3 seconds, returning to the starting position.

Benefits: Stretches all body muscles; tones the abdomen; strengthens calf muscles.

30. BHUJANG ASANA
(Cobra Pose)

✤ Lie on your stomach with your legs outstretched and heels together. Place your palms on the floor next to your chest, fingers pointing forward and elbows bent against your body.

✤ Inhale for 3 seconds, slowly raising your head, then neck, then shoulders, and then finally arching your back. Do not lift higher than the navel region and do not put pressure on your palms.

✤ Maintain this pose, holding your breath, for 6 seconds. Exhale for 3 seconds and return to the starting position.

Benefits: Increases breathing potential and stimulates circulation; promotes spinal flexibility and eases backache; tones reproductive organs and eases menstrual problems; relieves constipation.

31. DHANUR-VAKRA ASANA
(Bow Pose)

✤ Lie on your stomach with your legs slightly apart and arms at your sides. Bend your knees while reaching your hands back to take hold of your ankles.

✤ Inhale for 3 seconds, raising your neck and lifting your legs, thighs, and shoulders. Only your stomach remains on the floor.

✤ Maintain this pose, holding your breath, for 6 seconds. Exhale for 3 seconds and return to the starting position.

Benefits: Stretches the abdominal and pelvic muscles and spinal column; tones every part of the body; increases blood circulation to the abdominal region and sex organs.

32. ARDHA-MATSYENDRA ASANA
(Half Spinal Twist)

✤ Sit with your legs outstretched and bend your left leg, placing the foot beside your right hip. Place your right foot on the outside of your left knee, keeping the foot flat on the floor. Extend your left arm along the outside of your right calf, with your elbow at the knee, and grasp your right foot. Place your right arm behind your back.

✤ Exhale for 3 seconds, twisting your body from the waist toward the right. Maintain this pose, holding your breath, for 6 seconds. Inhale for 3 seconds and return to the starting position.

✤ Repeat for the other side.

Benefits: Helps correct spinal problems; increases flexibility.

33. HASTPAD-ANGUST ASANA I
(Extended Hand to Toe Pose I)

✤ Lie on your back, arms at your sides.

✤ Inhale for 2 seconds, raising your right arm straight up. Exhale for 2 seconds, raising your right leg straight up toward your right arm to touch your palm.

❖ Maintain this pose, holding your breath, for 4 seconds. Inhale for 2 seconds and return to the starting position. Repeat for the opposite side.

❖ Optional—Repeat, raising both arms and legs simultaneously.

Benefits: Improves circulation and strengthens abdominal muscles; massages internal abdominal organs; tones the lower back and lumbar spine; increases flexibility of the hips; strengthens the spine; increases body awareness, flexibility, concentration, and perseverance.

34. HASTPAD-ANGUST ASANA III
(Extended Hand to Toe Pose III)

❖ Lie on your back, arms outstretched at your sides, forming a T shape.

❖ Exhaling, lift your right leg, keeping your knee straight, and gently cross it over to the left side toward your left hand. (The twist in the body is felt in the lower spine.)

❖ Turn your head to the right and hold the pose. Then return to the starting position. Repeat for the opposite side.

Benefits: All the benefits of Hastpad-Angust Asana I.

35. HASTPAD-ANGUST ASANA II
(Extended Hand to Toe Pose II)

❖ Lie on your back, arms outstretched at your sides, forming a T shape.

❖ Exhale for 3 seconds, sliding your right leg toward your right arm as far as possible, or to hold your right toe.

❖ Maintain this pose, holding your breath, for 6 seconds. Inhale for 3 seconds and return to the starting position. Repeat for the opposite side.

Benefits: All the benefits of Hastpad-Angust Asana I.

36. HASTPAD-ANGUST ASANA IV
(Extended Hand to Toe Pose IV)

❖ Lie on one side and, exhaling for 2 seconds, raise your upper leg at a 90-degree angle. Raise your arm and take hold of your toe. Maintain the pose, holding your breath, for 4 seconds.

❖ Inhale for 2 seconds and return to the starting position. Repeat for the opposite side.

Benefits: All the benefits of Hastpad-Angust Asana I.

37. PARVAT ASANA IV
(Seated Mountain Pose IV)

✤ Sit in Sukh Asana (pose 3) or Padma Asana (pose 13), hands straight at your sides.

✤ Inhale for 3 seconds, raising both hands simultaneously and placing your palms together above your head. Keep your elbows straight and your arms close to your ears. Hold your back erect and tighten your abdomen slightly.

✤ Exhale for 3 seconds, twisting from the waist to the left side.

✤ Maintain this pose, holding your breath, for 6 seconds. Inhale for 3 seconds and return to the starting position. Repeat for the opposite side.

Benefits: Helps stiff shoulder and muscle aches; stretches the spine, hips, and shoulders; straightens back muscles; helps reduce fat around the abdomen; promotes stability, elevation, and self-expression.

38. HAMS ASANA
(Swan Pose)

✤ Sit on your heels, hands resting on your thighs. Exhale, sliding your hands down your thighs until your arms are fully extended. Keep your buttocks on your heels and rest your forehead on the floor, your chest on your thighs.

✤ Inhale, lifting your chest and coming to all fours. Exhale, lowering your body to the floor without moving your hands or knees.

✤ Return to the starting position.

Benefits: Relieves backache and strengthens the back muscles; brings humility.

39. PARYANK ASANA
(Couch Pose)

✤ Lie on your back with your legs outstretched and your hands locked on your abdomen. Breathe normally.

✤ Bend one leg outward to the side of your buttocks, toes out and heels touching the hip.

✤ Return to the starting position. Repeat for the opposite side.

Benefits: Stretches the inside of the leg; relieves pain in the hips and lower extremities; increases body awareness.

40. PAVAN-MUKTH ASANA
(Wind-Releasing Pose)

✤ Lie flat on your back with your legs fully outstretched, arms at your sides.

✤ Exhale for 2 seconds, raising your legs slowly and bending them so that your knees are close to your chest. Wrap your arms around your knees and squeeze into your chest.

✤ Maintain this pose, holding your breath, for 4 seconds. Inhale for 2 seconds and return to the starting position.

Benefits: Relieves gas and constipation; massages the abdominal organs.

41. PASCHI-MOTTANA ASANA
(Seated Forward Bend)

✤ Sit with your legs fully outstretched, toes pointing slightly inward.

✤ Inhale for 3 seconds, bringing your palms to your chest and drawing in your abdomen.

✤ Exhale for 3 seconds, bending forward and reaching out with your fingers or palms to touch your toes. Bring your head down to touch your knees.

✤ Maintain this pose, holding your breath, for 6 seconds. Inhale for 3 seconds and return to the starting position.

Benefits: Relieves constipation and stimulates the abdominal organs; preserves the normal elasticity of the spine; brings humility and relaxation.

42. USTRA ASANA
(Camel Pose)

✤ Sit on your heels with your hands on the floor behind you, on or near your toes, palms facing down. Inhale, arching your back while slowly lifting your pelvis. Gradually relax your head backward.

✤ Maintain this pose, holding your breath, for 6 seconds. Exhale for 3 seconds and return to the starting position.

Benefits: Stretches the anterior abdominal and upper thigh muscles; relaxes the neck and facial muscles; stimulates the thyroid gland, ovaries, and endocrine glands; accelerates circulation.

43. VAKRA ASANA III
(Twist Posture III)

✤ Lie on your back with your knees bent, heels and toes together, arms stretched out at the shoulder level, and palms facing upward.

✤ Exhaling, bend both legs from the knees to the left side, keeping your feet and knees aligned one on top of the other. While bending, turn your head to the right.

✤ Maintain this pose, holding your breath, for 4 seconds. Inhale for 2 seconds and return to the starting position. Repeat for the opposite side.

Benefits: Soothes the nerves; adjusts the vertebrae and lower back; relieves strain on the body.

44. HALA ASANA
(Plow Pose)

❖ Lie flat on your back with your legs outstretched and arms at your sides. Breathe deeply and regularly throughout the exercise.

❖ Keeping your knees straight, raise your legs to an angle of 30 degrees and hold the position for 5 seconds. Raise your legs another 30 degrees and hold for 5 seconds. Raise your legs until they are vertical. Hold for 2 seconds.

❖ Slowly swing your legs over your head to touch the floor with the tips of your toes. Slide your toes further away from your head and feel your weight shift toward the top of your spine. Hold the position for 15 to 20 seconds. Gradually reverse each step to return to the starting position.

Benefits: Stretches the spine and the abdominal muscles; improves circulation and thyroid function; prevents arthritis.

45. ARDH-SARVANG ASANA
(Half Shoulder Stand)

❖ Lie on your back with your legs outstretched and your hands on your hips.

❖ Inhaling and using the support of your hands against your hips, raise your legs together and slowly lift your body so that your buttocks rise straight up and the weight of your body rests on your shoulders and head.

❖ Bend at the knees and bring your heels to touch your buttocks. Hold the pose for a few seconds before inhaling and gradually returning to the starting position.

Benefits: Increases blood circulation to the upper parts of the body; strengthens the internal organs; relieves headache, congestion, and disorders of the ears, nose, and throat; stimulates sexuality.

46. SARVANG ASANA
(Shoulder Stand)

❖ Lie on your back with your legs outstretched and hands on your hips.

❖ Inhaling and using the support of your hands against your hips, raise your legs together and slowly lift your body so that your buttocks rise straight up and the weight of your body rests on your shoulders and head.

✤ Keep your legs and body straight. Hold the pose for a few seconds before inhaling and gradually returning to starting position.

Benefits: Increases blood circulation to the upper parts of the body; strengthens the internal organs; relieves headache, congestion, and disorders of the ears, nose, and throat; stimulates sexuality.

47. VRKS ASANA
(Tree Pose)

✤ Stand on your left leg with your foot firmly on the floor, hands on your hips. Focus on a spot in front of you.

✤ Inhale for 3 seconds, bending your right leg and placing the sole flat on your left inner thigh. Stretch your arms straight overhead and place your palms together. Maintain this pose, holding your breath, for 6 seconds. Exhale for 3 seconds and return to the starting position.

✤ Repeat for the opposite side.

Benefits: Tones the groin and inner thigh muscles; loosens the hip, knee, and ankle joints.

48. SIMHA ASANA
(Lion Pose)

✤ Kneel with your knees together and hands at your sides.

✤ Lower your buttocks to your heels and place your hands on your thighs.

✤ Lift your buttocks off your heels and raise your toes, letting your hands slide down and your fingers rest under your knees.

✤ Open your mouth and push your tongue down toward your chin; look at the tip of your nose. Hold the position for 10 seconds, inhaling and exhaling through your mouth.

Benefits: Relaxes the face and smoothes wrinkles; strengthens the voice and helps sore throat.

49. VAJRA ASANA
(Thunderbolt Pose)

✤ Kneel with your knees together, heels apart, and hands at your sides.

✤ Lower your buttocks between your heels and rest your hands on your knees.

✤ Hold your neck and body erect and your spine straight.

Benefits: Corrects posture; increases flexibility

in the ankles and feet; relaxes the thigh muscles; improves digestion; helps prepare for meditation and maintain emotional control.

50. MAKRA ASANA
(*Crocodile Pose*)

❖ Lie on your stomach with your hands folded under your head. Your abdomen and front of your body should be touching the ground, legs fully outstretched, with some distance between them.

❖ Close your eyes. Relax completely and remain motionless. Breathe normally and clear your head of all thoughts.

❖ Remain in this position for 10 to 15 minutes.
Benefits: Refreshes the mind and body; relieves strain, fatigue, and mental stress.

51. DRADH ASANA
(*Firm Side Pose*)

❖ Lie on your right side with your body completely relaxed and your right arm under your head (as if for a pillow). Keep your legs straight, one over the other.

❖ Close your eyes and empty your mind of all thoughts.

❖ Repeat on the opposite side.

Benefits: Eases stress and improves breathing; offers good relaxation.

52. NISHPAND-BHAV ASANA
(*Relaxation Pose*)

❖ Sit with your back against a wall, legs apart at a comfortable distance, and hands lying loosely on your legs.

❖ Sit motionless, close your eyes, and feel calm while breathing normally. Focus your attention on a sound (preferably a rhythmic peaceful sound).

❖ Sit passively in this position for 10 minutes, completely focused on the sound.
Benefits: Releases tension; induces physical relaxation and mental tranquillity.

53. SHAV ASANA
(*Corpse Pose*)

❖ Lie on your back with your feet and arms apart at a comfortable distance. Remain motionless, closing your eyes and relaxing your body to a listless state. Breathe normally.

❖ Focus on different parts of your body, starting with your toes, to check for relaxation.

❖ Remain in this position for 5 to 15 minutes.

Benefits: Provides an ideal ending to the yoga exercise; induces better sleep; regulates energy equally among body parts; provides good muscular relaxation, and calms the mind.

What Is Pranayam?
Pranayam is the "breathing process" or the control of the motion of inhalation, and exhalation, and the retention of vital energy. The success of pranayam depends on maintaining the proper ratio of inhalation, exhalation, and retention.

Benefits of Pranayam
During pranayam, inhalation stimulates the system and fills the lungs with fresh air; retention raises the internal temperature of the body and plays an important part in increasing the absorption of oxygen; exhalation causes the diaphragm to return to its original position, forcing out air that is full of toxins and impurities by contracting intercostal muscles. These are the main components of pranayam that massage the abdominal muscles and facilitate the functioning of the various organs of the body. With the proper functioning of these organs, vital energy flows to all the systems. The practice of pranayam is known to prevent many serious illnesses.

54. PRANAYAM I
(Breathing I)
✢ Stand erect in a relaxed, comfortable posture with your feet apart, arms at your sides.
✢ Inhale slowly and comfortably to the best count for you (start with 4 seconds and increase by 1 second every week). Use all your respiratory muscles and avoid jerky movements.
✢ Exhale slowly to the same count as the inhalation. Repeat a few times.

55. PRANAYAM II
(Breathing II)
✢ Sit or stand erect and place your hands just below your ribs with your thumbs facing backward.
✢ Inhale for 4 seconds by expanding the muscles between your ribs. (Try to expand your chest sideways. Concentrate on the lower part of your ribs—feel your lungs expand and try not to use your abdominal or collarbone muscles.)
✢ Exhale for 4 seconds to return to the starting position. Repeat a few times.

56. PRANAYAM III
(Breathing III)

❖ Sit or stand erect and place your fingers on your collarbone muscles.

❖ Inhale for 2 seconds, lifting your shoulders slightly up and backward. (Use only the collarbone muscles, not the abdominal muscles.)

❖ Exhale for 2 seconds, bringing your shoulders forward and down. Repeat a few times.

57. PRANAYAM IV
(Breathing IV)

❖ Lie on your back with your knees pulled up, feet together near your buttocks. Place one hand on your abdomen.

❖ Inhale for 3 seconds, moving only your abdominal muscles upward.

❖ Exhale for 3 seconds, moving your abdominal muscles downward. Repeat a few times.

58. PRANAYAM V
(Breathing V)

❖ Sit in Sukh Asana (pose 3) or another meditative posture.

❖ Close your left nostril with your finger and inhale for 2 seconds through your right nostril. Close both nostrils with your thumb and little finger and hold your breath for 4 seconds. Exhale through your left nostril.

❖ Close your right nostril with your finger and inhale for 2 seconds through your left nostril.

❖ Again close both nostrils with your thumb and little finger and hold your breath for 4 seconds. Exhale through your right nostril. Repeat the whole cycle, starting with closing your right nostril.

59. RELAXING EYES

❖ Sit in a comfortable position with your gaze fixed on a candle flame (alternatively, look at your thumb).

❖ Gaze as long as possible without blinking. If your eyes start watering, stop.

❖ Close your eyes and rub your hands together to warm your palms. Place them over your eyelids. Relax.

60. RELAXING EARS

✤ Hold your ears between your thumbs and index fingers.

✤ Apply pressure, massaging both ears at the same time, front and back.

✤ Massage for 1 minute.

61. RELAXING NECK AND SHOULDERS

✤ Bend your head to the left, pushing your left shoulder down. Bend your head to the right side, pushing your right shoulder down.

✤ Lean your head back and hold that position for 20 seconds. Bend your head forward and hold for 20 seconds.

✤ Allow your head to sink forward and rotate it slowly. Repeat a few times.

62. RELAXING TONGUE

✤ Close your lips and explore the insides of your mouth with the tip of your tongue for 30 seconds.

✤ Use the tip of your tongue to apply pressure at the center of your upper palate for 15 seconds.

✤ Alternatively, imagine sucking a lemon and continue this motion for 30 seconds.

Index